D0966769

REBOOTING

For further information:

The Kabbalah Centre
155 E. 48th St., New York, NY 10017
1062 S. Robertson Blvd., Los Angeles, CA 90035

1.800.Kabbalah
www.kabbalah.com

First Edition
January 2007
Printed in USA
ISBN10: 1-57189-560-4
ISBN13: 978-1-57189-560-8

Design: HL Design (Hyun Min Lee) www.hldesignco.com

www.kabbalah.com™

REBOOTING

DEFEATING DEPRESSION WITH THE POWER OF KABBALAH

TECHNOLOGY FOR THE SOUL™   YEHUDA BERG

ACKNOWLEDGMENTS

To the people who make my life better each and every day: my parents, the Rav and Karen; my brother Michael; my wife Michal and our children; and my dear friend Billy.

REBOOTING

TABLE OF CONTENTS

REBOOTING

FOREWORD

On September 2, 2004, my father, teacher, friend, and at times even my identity and my world, had a stroke. In the beginning, the doctors said that the Rav would not survive. He did. They said that he would not talk or walk. He is walking and talking. But for me, my family, and countless others, the loss of the old Rav, as we knew him, created a black hole through which we try to bravely navigate each day, just as he does.

It was a moment that shook us all, and the aftermath of the Rav's stroke continues to shape and change us. Each person in our large family of supporters has suffered from the Rav's illness in his or her own private way. For the Kabbalah Centre as a whole and for the hundreds of thousands of people who study Kabbalah, Kabbalist Rav Berg represented an unshakable strength and power that lay beyond physicality. He was our modern-day superhero—one who effortlessly traversed the spiritual and physical terrain of this universe.

The number of miracles that the Rav helped people achieve in their lives is too many to record in any book. Today, however, it is the Rav who is the miracle. He walks and talks and teaches. But the Rav is still not the same Rav I knew. Those of us who have experienced his strength and wisdom can't help but wonder, how could this happen to someone as extraordinary as the Rav?

But it did. And unexpected change is difficult for almost anyone—no matter how spiritually adept that individual is. For that reason, there are those who now choose to question the system, the Centre, and the Rav. On the other hand, there are individuals who continue to study and to experience the blessings that Kabbalah brings to their lives—blessings that the Rav helped make accessible to millions. The Rav has quietly transformed from a real live superhero at the forefront of a movement into a historic man in the background who once did something that had never been done before.

For me, my father just left. Throughout all my years in Kabbalah, I have been surrounded by this magnificent system and by my amazing, loving, and powerful parents, who raised me along a path that I loved with a destiny that was ready for me to take. So when my father left, for the first time in my life I felt alone, with a big, ugly black hole that I now had to face every morning of every waking day.

And every waking day I asked myself, why? Why did the Rav leave me? It would be some time before I understood that it was not personal.

It took me several months before I stopped operating on autopilot and moved out of the abandonment phase into the next phase of my grief—the phase in which I was forced to really deal with what had happened. And it was the most painful thing I had ever experienced—a pain I know many kabbalists in history experienced when they too lost their teacher. My father himself was one such student who lost his teacher years ago and suffered greatly as a result.

My cave was a dark, empty one in which no hope could dwell. I was DEPRESSED. My depression was compounded by the expectation that I placed on myself and that I felt from others, which was that I wasn't supposed to be susceptible to depression. I had all the tools at my disposal to bounce back, right?

It took me almost two years to research and write this book, and it was while doing this work that I really began to understand what had happened on that life-changing day. That day was the beginning of an entire chapter—my first real test of how the system of Kabbalah works. Writing this book helped me face the pain, wake up from shutting down, and see what the Rav's illness had come to teach me. I could not have written this book or shared this wisdom with people in such a sincere and honest way if I had not gone through the darkness myself. I have experienced firsthand what I discuss in this book, and I have used the tools that I suggest. And it's through the process of using the tools and sharing that I am on the other side of depression today.

The work that my brother and I have done since the Rav had his stroke, the way the Centre has grown as a whole—none of it would ever have happened if the Rav were still doing it all for us. After all, when there's a superhero around, you get a little lazy and let him do all the work. But the truth is that we all need to be our own superhero. That is what Kabbalah says, and that is what the Rav always wanted. I'll be the first one to tell you that becoming your own superhero is hard. My mother always said that it takes a lot of pressure to turn a piece of coal into a brilliant diamond. And I'll be honest—I was not ready for that type of pressure. But today I see the brilliance in the plan.

I hope that this book and the tools included within it, as well as my personal story of how the process of Kabbalah brought me out of my pain, are a gift for you. May they help guide you safely through the darkness to find your own divine brilliance.

That is my hope. That is my purpose. And I believe in my heart that it remains the goal of the Rav as well.

—YEHUDA BERG, Los Angeles, CA, January 2007

INTRODUCTION

This is a book about love and Light and freedom from depression. Many of you who are reading this may feel that you can never be free from depression, but that's the illness talking. In point of fact, you can. And Kabbalah can give you the tools to reboot your life. Kabbalah is known as a 4,000-year-old body of wisdom that addresses both the spiritual and physical laws of this world. I like to think of it as a technology for life, because it is grounded in principles that can be scientifically proven and are also highly effective on a practical level. Kabbalah teaches us that unconditional joy and uninhibited bliss are everywhere; in fact, they are the internal software that operates this universe. Rocks, trees, our pets, our parents, the air, and even our own bodies and souls—all have a profound and lasting happiness at their very core. This means that we all carry within us the very healing that we are seeking; all we need to do is learn how to access it.

One of my favorite kabbalistic stories is that of Rav Akiva. Rav Akiva lived in the second century and was a very, very negative man. If it was sunny out, he would complain that his throat was parched and that he could never find shade. If it was raining, he would complain that the world was becoming dank. Despite his negative outlook, a wise and compassionate woman fell in love with him. She tried to persuade him to change his ways and to view life more charitably. "When the sun is out and your throat is dry," the woman said to Rav Akiva, "this dryness

INTRODUCTION   3 creates a desire for drink. Drink can be pleasurable and satisfying, and it can also prompt you to meet with friends and drink together. So a pleasant gathering of souls can be brought about by your parched throat."

"But I don't have any friends," Rav Akiva said.

"Without the sun," the woman continued, "the plants would wither and we would go hungry. So isn't a little discomfort worth a lifetime of nourishment?" But Rav Akiva would have nothing to do with this way of thinking. "I am 40 years old," he would say. "It's too late, and I'm too evil."

But the woman would not be dissuaded by Rav Akiva's negative disposition. She led him through a meadow where she stopped and pointed to a modest stream where the water had carved a hole through the rock. Rav Akiva had never been particularly drawn to beauty before, but suddenly he understood the significance of what he was seeing. "If something as soft as water has worn a hole in something as hard as stone," he said aloud, "then I too must be able to take my positive traits and use them to wear a hole in my negative ones. I too must be able to transform." After this realization—this great moment of clarity—Rav Akiva was gradually able to transform his negative qualities. He went on to become one of the highest souls and most influential teachers who ever lived.

INTRODUCTION

This story should serve as an inspiration for anyone who is on a spiritual path, but I feel it is a particularly powerful metaphor for those who are suffering from depression—because it teaches us that we too can transform seemingly insurmountable, painful, or debilitating thoughts into positive energy. We too can convert darkness into light. The key is that Rav Akiva didn't change overnight. His transformation was a process. He had to initiate a series of sometimes small and sometimes large steps before his darkness dissipated and his suffering gave way to peace and joy.

Now is a perfect time for me to emphasize the importance of having realistic expectations. Profound change rarely happens with one "aha" moment; more typically, it is a continuous process in which the gentle motion and constant cleansing of water wears away the rock that is our negativity.

I am not a medical doctor, but I am drawn to the topic of depression and believe that the information provided in this book will help shine a kabbalistic light on this all-too-common disorder. I am also convinced that through the practice of Kabbalah, those of us who suffer from depression—no matter where we are, what we've done, what faith we follow, or how educated we may be—can defeat this condition if we just take the time to understand its true source. Conventional methods for treating depression attempt to control its symptoms, an approach that certainly has its merits. Kabbalah, however, provides the tools to truly face the challenge of depression on a daily basis and beat it. Kabbalah uncovers depression at its very root.

From a kabbalistic point of view, I want to point out that there is a difference between sadness and depression. Sadness may well accompany depression, but it is not the same thing. Perhaps you might think it unnecessary to define sadness. After all, everyone knows what it means to feel sad, right? But do we really? Kabbalah says that people experience sadness in different ways. Moreover, some people go through life so far removed from their emotions that they might not even recognize what sadness or happiness feels like. Fortunately, the kabbalistic wisdom that can be found in this book can help us get back in touch with the multitude of emotions that make life worth living. And believe it or not, sadness is one of the most important of these emotions.

So what is real sadness? Sadness is:

- A natural and healthy reaction to a painful experience.

- A short-lived process that passes as you address and transform the circumstances that caused your experience.

- Essential to spiritual and emotional growth.

Unlike sadness, depression is **not** one of the steps to personal development, although you will grow by leaps and bounds when you use the tools of Kabbalah to overcome it. Depression is a pervasive feeling of physical and emotional numbness or fog. Depression feels like a tunnel with no light at the end, or a dark cave that lacks any illumination. Kabbalistically speaking, depression is an absence of desire. We'll talk more about this very important point in a moment.

Depression arises when we constantly feel like victims of our experience rather than directors of our lives—when we feel helpless and hopeless about our ability to effect change. Depression rears its ugly head when we don't want to face our "garbage"—those unconstructive aspects of ourselves that are crying out to be noticed and turned into gifts. We all have these types of traits, and most of us would prefer to ignore them. But depression is a sign that the cost of doing so has become too great—that it's time for a change. And Kabbalah is meant to be a technology to help you make such a transformation.

We need specific tools to help us regain a sense of being the cause of the events in our lives rather than merely the effect. We need tools to help us convert our garbage into assets that bring us lasting joy. In the pages that lie ahead, Kabbalah will provide just such tools. In fact, you will find in this book an abundance of practical strategies with which to lift yourself out of the fog that is depression, as well as valuable techniques that will allow you to connect to a constant stream of life-affirming, positive energy. Think of Kabbalah as the software to the "restart" key. My goal in this book is to encourage and empower you to push the button and take back the life that is yours.

A BRIEF LINEAGE

The wisdom in this book has been passed down to me by my father, Rav Berg. When I was young, Rav Berg would spend countless hours teaching my brother and me the ancient wisdom that is Kabbalah. We would stay up past dawn reading various texts and discussing them—sometimes heatedly—only to have to attend school the following morning! My mother has also been instrumental in my spiritual education, as well as in the spiritual education of countless others. She has opened many doors, making the wisdom of Kabbalah accessible to the world. It is her giving and open heart that has instilled within me an understanding and a passion for helping people. And it is the wisdom that my father has selflessly imparted to me over the years that inspires me to share what I have learned from him .

The changes I have experienced within myself because of Kabbalah have been profound and lasting. That is because Kabbalah itself is profound and lasting. In fact, its teachings are more than 4,000 years old. They began with Abraham, who is considered to be the father of Judaism, Christianity, and Islam. I point out this shared lineage to emphasize that Kabbalah is for everyone. Although there are some who believe that Kabbalah is only for those of the Jewish faith, it is in fact intended for all the people of the world. In no way does Kabbalah challenge or replace faith; instead, it serves only to enhance it. I emphasize this point because I don't want anyone to miss out on the gifts that Kabbalah has to offer by virtue of any confusion or misconception in this regard.

Before we move ahead, I want to mention that for many years, the wisdom of Kabbalah was kept secret. Only prominent male scholars were permitted access to kabbalistic books and teachings. In the 20th century, a great kabbalist and scholar, Rav Yehuda Ashlag, deciphered these texts, making them accessible to all. He then passed the teachings down to Rav Yehuda Brandwein, who in turn passed them down to my father. Each of these pioneering scholars suffered greatly for having gone against the prevailing belief that Kabbalah's teachings should be limited to only a few. Despite relentless opposition and torment, Rav Brandwein, my father, and my mother came to the conclusion that with proper education and support, Kabbalah could be of benefit to everyone—especially to those of us who have lost a sense of hope and a desire for life.

As you turn the pages of this book, you may be struck by the notion that you have always known what you have just read but have not been able to articulate it. This is because the contents of this book represent universal truths about human nature. So take your time with these concepts; mull them over, test them out, and see how they actually work. Think of the process as an art class: Would you believe that yellow and red mixed together make orange simply because your art teacher told you so? No, you would probably want to grab hold of those paint tubes and see for yourself! You might make a mess, and the paint may splatter, but tidiness is not the goal. It is the process itself—the act of discovery—that is your spiritual path out of depression.

When the text feels challenging, I encourage you to hang on through these moments. You can also call our support line at 1-800-KABBALAH. The goal here is not just to help you cope with depression, but to defeat it once and for all. Accomplishing this goal will require you to stretch in some places. I hope you will find encouragement in knowing that your efforts will be rewarded with the greatest gift you can imagine: regaining your appetite for living.

PART ONE

DEPRESSION, ITS SYMPTOMS, AND THE POWER TO OVERCOME THEM

If you suffer from depression, know that you are not alone. When I first decided to write this book, I did quite a bit of research and discovered that about 18.8 million Americans, or 9.5% of the U.S. population, suffer from depression each year. And this staggering number represents only those who have actively sought help; millions of others remain undiagnosed. I also learned that women are twice as likely as men to become depressed, and that while depression may strike at any age— from childhood right through to our retirement years—it is most common during the onset of early middle age. Depression knows no distinctions of race or social status. The majority of people who attempt or commit suicide have been struggling unsuccessfully with depression for years.

I learned that depression can manifest in a myriad of forms, often traveling in tandem with anxiety. According to research, depression and anxiety are both reactions to fear. The difference is that with anxiety, our "fight-or-flight" survival mechanism goes into overdrive, whereas with depression we suppress our responses altogether.

The symptoms of depression can be arranged into five categories.

1. Physical:

- Loss of appetite or increased appetite, resulting in unusual weight loss or weight gain.

- Lethargy to a degree that even the smallest task seems utterly overwhelming, and the body seems to resist activity of any kind.

- Chronic ailments that don't respond to treatment, such as headaches, stomach aches, and back pain.

- Worsening of preexisting conditions such as rheumatoid arthritis or diabetes.

- Slowed speech and movements, as if one is wading through mud.

2. Emotional:

- Persistent sadness or numbness.

- Restlessness, agitation, anxiety, or irritability.

- An overwhelming sense of guilt, worthlessness, and helplessness.

3. Behavioral:

- Loss of interest in pleasurable activities, including sex.

- Insomnia, early-morning awakening, or oversleeping.

- Isolation from friends and family.

- Drug or alcohol abuse.

4. Cognitive:

- Difficulty concentrating.

- Poor memory skills.

- Trouble making decisions.

5. Spiritual:

- Feelings of hopelessness, loss of joy, or pessimism.

- Lack of desire to change or grow.

- Lack of meaning and purpose.

- Preoccupation with death or suicide.

Almost everyone has experienced one or more of these symptoms at some point in their lives. It would be very difficult to be human and *not* have days when you eat too much, a weekend where you hole up in your bedroom, or lose your cool with your kids or the clerk at the DMV. This does *not* mean that you are depressed. However, if you are experiencing five or more of these symptoms consistently over an extended period of time, then you might be struggling with some form of depression.

As I continued with my research, I found that depression takes a variety of forms. Here are some of the most common.

Major Depression. This is the most severe form of depression. A single traumatic event can trigger it, or it may develop slowly as a consequence of a series of disappointments or life problems. Sometimes it's difficult to pinpoint a cause at all. If you suffer from major depression, there is likely to be a noticeable change in your daily routine as well as a loss of interest in activities that you once enjoyed. For example, you might be an avid pet lover, but you no longer look forward to walking your dog. Or perhaps you're a loving parent but lately find yourself staying in bed in the middle of the afternoon rather than interacting with your children.

Dysthymia. This chronic, low-level form of depression is also known as "mild depression," and it often persists for years. As a sufferer, you might not remember a time when you *didn't* feel depressed. Although dysthymia can affect your quality of life, your ability to participate in your usual work, family, and social activities generally remains outwardly unchanged. This makes dysthymia easy to overlook.

Adjustment Disorder. This is a mild form of depression resulting from a specific trauma, such as a relationship breakup, loss of a job, or death of a loved one. While most people experience sadness during such events, those with adjustment disorder take longer than expected to adjust to the change. If you suffer from adjustment disorder, your ability to participate in daily activities will often be affected as well.

Bipolar Disorder (Manic Depression). Those with Bipolar Disorder experience low lows and manic highs in often bewildering cycles.

These mood swings can be mild, moderate, or severe. During a manic phase, you might experience exaggerated feelings of well-being mixed with tremendous bursts of activity. During a depressive phase, it is sometimes difficult even to get out of bed in the morning.

Seasonal Affective Disorder (SAD). SAD is also known as "winter blues" and is associated with sunlight deprivation. One conventional method of treatment involves the use of sunlamps.

Premenstrual Dysphoric Disorder (PMDD). PMDD is a severe form of the more commonly recognized condition known as premenstrual syndrome. If you're a women who suffers from PMDD, you might experience debilitating bouts of depression in the second half of your cycle. These episodes usually subside at the onset of menstruation or shortly thereafter.

Postpartum Depression. This type of depression has received increased media attention in the past few years. It encompasses all the symptoms of depression but may also include excessive preoccupation with an infant's health or consistent thoughts of harming the baby. It can last for up to one year after the child's birth.

Psychotic Depression. In addition to many of the symptoms of depression, psychotic depression may also include hallucinations or delusions. In most cases, those who suffer from this form of depression recognize that their delusionary thoughts do not reflect reality.

Atypical Depression. Despite its name, this is actually the most common form of depression. If you struggle with atypical depression, you might notice that you are able to experience temporary relief from depressed thinking, usually in response to a positive life event.

Agitated Depression. In addition to experiencing the classic symptoms of depression, those with agitated depression are usually restless, unable to sit in one place, or incapable of focusing on a task to completion. For this reason, they tend to occupy their minds with trivial, short-term tasks.

This is by no means an exhaustive list of the forms depression can take. Other variations undoubtedly exist, since this is an illness that is as individual as those who suffer from it. Just because what you're experiencing is not listed here does not mean it's any less troublesome. The good news is that the tools discussed in this book apply to any and all forms of depression.

A BRIEF HISTORY OF DEPRESSION

Historically, depression has been understood in two very different ways. In so-called primitive cultures, mental illness was often ascribed to an external force or presence. Blame might be placed on a witch who had cast a spell on the sufferer, for example, or on a succubus who had visited the victim during the night. In such contexts, the source of mental illness was always perceived to be something that had entered the person's consciousness from the outside. Kabbalah also speaks about this possibility, which we'll discuss in more detail later on.

By the end of the 19th century, many in the scientific community had begun to discredit the notion that emotional disturbances were caused by an external agent. Instead, they began to view depression as a disruption of the body's normal neurological function, or as an indicator of repressed memories, frightening desires, or psychosexual trauma. Therapies influenced by Sigmund Freud shared the assumption that depression, anxiety, and other sorts of despair all originated within the psyche. This shifted the focus from an external source to an internal one, which is where the field of psychology still lingers today.

Currently there are a variety of therapies available to help deal with depression. These include psychoanalysis, cognitive rehabilitation, behavior modification, talk therapy, biofeedback, art therapy, and a plethora of bodywork. But it is medication that has become one of the most popular therapeutic tools in use today. The most common of these is the class of drugs known as SSRI's, or selective serotonin reuptake inhibitor. Currently, nearly 33% of Americans who are taking antidepressants are experiencing some degree of relief from their symptoms.

Each of the treatment methods outlined above does have its merits. Used individually or in combination, they can allow us to interact more easily with the world, thereby significantly contributing to our mental health. From a kabbalistic standpoint, however, such treatments target only the *effects* of depression while ignoring its root cause. Don't get me wrong; we are very fortunate to have such a profound awareness of depression and so many means available to us to address its symptoms. We have made huge progress from a time, as recent as half a century ago, when those suffering from depression were shunned, treated like lepers, and sent to live in sanatoriums. But there is still much work to be done.

Many people experiencing depression remain afraid to seek help, embarrassed by the stigma that still attaches to any kind of illness affecting the mind. Some turn to their family physicians, who, if not properly educated in detecting depression, may pre-scribe drugs that combat its symptoms—this drug for insom-nia, that one for appetite suppression, and so on—without ever dealing with the root issue. Some individuals do find proper diagnosis and care from qualified professionals, but all too often the benefits prove temporary. This means that while most people do recover from their initial depressive episode, the recurrence rate remains high, approaching 60% within two years and 75% within ten years. Why does depression tend to recur? Because conventional treatments do no more than help patients *adapt* to their condition. Thankfully, however, there is an alternative.

If you are really serious about overcoming depression, you can go beyond merely coping. You can go beyond just controlling depressive symptoms. A more joyful space for living does exist. This approach is very much akin to what alternative health practitioners teach about the importance of preventive health measures: that if we all regularly practiced healthy ways of liv-ing, we would need hospitals only for emergencies such as the mending of sprained limbs in ski accidents or playground high jinks. In much the same way, if we take the time to look at the source of our depression now, we can spare ourselves the fig-urative trip to the emergency room later on.

Which brings us to the question:

REBOOTING

What lies at the root of depression?

LOSS OF DESIRE

According to conventional medicine, one of the outcomes of depression is a lack of desire. In other words, lack of desire is an effect of depression, according to many doctors. The conventional medical model tells us that when we are depressed, we subsequently lose desire not only for our basic needs, such as food, sleep, work, and cleanliness, but also for things that once excited us—activities such as long runs, travel, knitting, crossword puzzles, sex, political activism, or watching our favorite NFL team play on Sundays. According to the prevailing approach toward depression, if we treat the depression, the desire for these activities will inevitably return, and any other negative by-products will eventually dissipate as well.

But according to Kabbalah, conventional medicine has it backwards. And this is why:

Kabbalistically, lack of desire is the cause of depression and not the effect.

REBOOTING

To be absolutely clear here . . .

The lack of desire comes first; it's the root of the problem.

From this perspective, we don't need to set off on a long and difficult quest to cure our depression in order to feel desire again. On the contrary, *we can fight and overcome our depression by bringing desire back into our lives.* This is a dramatic, exciting, and ultimately empowering distinction. If we are depressed and believe we need to overcome our depression in order to reignite our desire, we might spend many years searching for the source of our depression. But with this new kabbalistic perspective, we already know the source of our problem: We have lost our desire. The amazing news is that this is a state we can remedy. After all, simply knowing what we have to do takes us halfway to our goal. And, as it happens, there are many actions we can take to reconnect with our desire. When you reconnect with desire, you reconnect with life and with all of its depth and richness. Before we delve into specific strategies, however, let's discuss desire in more detail.

Desire often gets a bad rap. Many people believe that in order to be on a spiritual path, one must first be free of desire—that desire itself is what wreaks so much havoc in our lives. Nothing could be further from the truth. According to Kabbalah, desire is the most important force in our daily lives. It is what animates us, and it is therefore essential to our existence. It is our desire for water that causes us to go about finding ourselves something to drink; our desire for rest that leads us to find a means for sleep; our desire for love that causes us to search for a partner; and our desire for greatness that prompts us to overcome seemingly insurmountable obstacles in order to accomplish great things. Even the desires that lead us astray are vital to our path—for without them, we would never grow and change.

Desire leads to action. We wouldn't lift a finger if we didn't desire something. Depression arises when we lose contact with our desire, and this is what we are here both to explore and to remedy.

Kabbalah tells us that there are four levels of desire:

1. No desire at all.

2. Trying: We're giving it a shot, but not with everything we've got.

3. Going the extra mile: We're making a sincere effort and keeping focused on the goal.

4. Making it happen no matter what: We do everything in our power to attain the object of our desire. No other result will do.

REBOOTING

Most people function at the level of trying, occasionally mustering the energy to push toward level three. But those of us who are afflicted with depression are stuck at level one. We are living at a level of consciousness in which no desire exists at all. And this is merely existing, not living, because joy cannot arise in the absence of desire. When there is no joy, we feel as though we are living in darkness.

The question becomes, how do we rid ourselves of the darkness? It's simple. How do you transform a dark room? You switch on the light, of course. The light allows us to see the varied colors and textures of a room that no more than a second ago was shrouded in black. In a brightly lit room, real living can commence. In kabbalistic terms, the light that has the power to illuminate a dim room is a metaphor for something much more brilliant.

The Light, according to Kabbalah, is every positive emotion and every blissful moment you can possibly imagine, and it flows directly from our Creator. This means that we have an endless supply of this amazing stuff, and we just need to find the light switch in order to activate it. The good news is that this goal is much closer than you might think. In fact, the key to conquering depression has been right under your nose all along. That's because the cure for depression presents itself to us in the form of our daily struggles.

Yes, our daily struggles.

Minor and not-so-minor mishaps. Difficult interactions with children, spouses, and friends. Work deadlines. Experiences that just don't feel easy. You know what I'm talking about. Believe it or not, it is these struggles that provide the very fodder we need to transform our personal pain into unconditional and limitless joy. Without fertile soil, there is nowhere for a seed to grow. And the beauty of it is that our daily challenges are perfectly designed to maximize our spiritual and emotional growth.

Needless to say, we don't always handle our day-to-day hurdles with the grace we would like to muster. Sometimes we fall short of our own expectations or those that others have for us. Sometimes we feel as if we have failed, and perhaps this sense of failure is what caused our depression in the first place. According to Kabbalah, however, part of our purpose as human beings is to fall.

What do I mean by falling? Falling is saying or doing something hurtful—cheating, not being honest, gossiping about a friend or a relative, or making poor choices that affect others. In other words, falling is making a mistake—the sort of mistake every human being makes. Yes, every human being—even the great kabbalists.

Although falling down may feel uncomfortable and even painful at times, there is a great deal of beauty in it—*if* we make the choice to learn from our mistakes and move past them. In this way, falling actually gives us the opportunity to grow and develop, as well as to be more than we were before we fell. It's really the only way we have to move forward.

Think about this for a moment. It's a simple thought, but it's also one of the greatest truths I've learned—a truth my parents taught me, and one that dramatically changed my life:

Every time we fall and get back up, we create a greater capacity for joy, or Light, to enter our lives.

In fact, the process of falling, brushing ourselves off, and moving on brings in more Light than would be manifest had we not fallen at all. In the face of this all-powerful Light, the darkness of our depression will cease to exist. The truth of the matter is that there is no such thing as failure when we view our mistakes as part of the growth process rather than expecting perfection from ourselves. In Kabbalah, there are no mistakes—only opportunities.

SAM'S STORY

One of the women who works at The Kabbalah Centre in Los Angeles has a son whom we'll call Sam. Sam was a terrible procrastinator. When he was in seventh grade, he fell so far behind in his homework that he needed to complete 25 assignments just to catch up. The enormity of this task plunged Sam into depression. He couldn't stop berating himself over how badly he had messed up. What a terrible mistake he had made by getting himself into this mess! He convinced himself that he was a bad person and began to lose sight of his gifts, as well as the opportunity that the situation presented to him. As is the case with so many of us in the throes of depression, Sam felt incapable of doing anything to help himself, so his situation only got worse. But his mother explained to him that if he just put some effort into completing those assignments, no matter how burdensome they might seem, Sam would draw Light into his life.

His mom was exactly right, and here's why:

As I mentioned earlier, we are all chock-full of desires, and these desires are essential to living. In fact, our Creator designed us solely as creatures of desire. We were made to be like a cup—or, in the language of Kabbalah, a Vessel—that is constantly yearning to be filled. This Vessel, which *is* perpetual yearning, is called Desire to Receive. In kabbalistic terms, our desire is our Vessel. The bigger our desire, the bigger our Vessel, and vice versa. Again, it's just like a cup: The larger our cup, the more thirst-quenching refreshment the cup can hold.

But unlike a cup, which one typically fills with tangible substances, our cravings turn out to be directed toward intangibles: things like happiness and love, pleasure and excitement, security and comfort. We crave the good stuff but don't know where to find it. Unbeknownst to most of us, however, we have access to it 24/7. It comes in the form of the Light, which we touched on earlier and will spend more time discussing in Part Two. And the bigger our Vessel, the greater will be our capacity to hold Light. When we expand our Vessel by facing a challenge head-on, we increase the amount of divine energy that flows into our cup. Our desire grows, and the Light rushes in to fill it. And since lack of desire causes depression, increasing desire will inevitably lead to the defeat of depression.

Conversely, we have the power to shrink our Vessel, and with it our desire. That's what we do every time we are confronted with a challenge and choose to shrink from it in fear. When we shut down completely and go into "avoidance mode," our desire shrivels up, and we cut ourselves off from the influx of life-affirming Light. Our potential for fulfillment then takes a nose-dive, and we are reduced to a state of darkness.

But when we face a situation directly and resist the urge to shut down, we become the cause of our own destiny rather than remaining an effect, a mere victim of circumstance. We become more like the Creator, the cause of all great things. And the more our actions mirror those of the Creator, the more Light of the Creator we will bring into our world. Why? Because of the Law of Attraction, which states that *like attract like*. If you behave like the Creator, you receive what the Creator offers: divine satisfaction in the form of Light.

DARKNESS CANNOT EXIST WHERE THERE IS LIGHT.

If that weren't enough, there is yet another bonus that comes with confronting adversity and bringing Light into an otherwise gray, muted world. Once you recognize the power of your choices and choose to move forward, your self-esteem grows. With every proactive step you take, you feel more and more capable as a human being, because you see how much you *can* do rather than being inhibited by what you feel you *can't* do. Just one step activates and enhances the Light within you. But these steps don't have to be huge leaps or bounds; even baby steps will do. With each step your confidence grows, and you move closer and closer to your true potential.

Remember that greatness is not a result of what you achieve in life; it is a result of what you overcome. There are countless people who achieve great success in their lives, but many of them remain plagued by insecurity and anxiety. Conversely, people who have faced adversity and have learned to overcome it become wise and secure within themselves as a result.

The key lies in beginning the process from exactly where you are in this moment. Once you take the first step, you activate the Light; you flip on the light switch, so to speak. Your world becomes brighter *instantaneously*. The hard part is taking that first step. But don't worry; we'll show you exactly how to make forward progress, no matter what your circumstance may be.

Now let's get back to Sam's story. With his mother's encouragement, Sam went to work. In the beginning he experienced little joy, but after having caught up on his third or fourth assignment, Sam's desire to complete all of his assignments became activated. He began to feel capable and, by extension, saw his own inherent value as a human being. He experienced his true creativity and skill. After finishing half of his assignments, he started to feel truly good about himself. And by the time he had caught up with all of his work, he had acquired a newfound respect for his own power and had begun to feel increasingly confident that he could face other challenges as well. And now, each time Sam decides to stand back up after a fall, he will draw more Light.

Another vital lesson Sam learned is that it's okay to make mistakes. In point of fact, the entire purpose of life is to make mistakes—to fall, to learn, and to grow. It is in our nature to feel shame and guilt about our weaknesses—but once we recognize that our negative traits are actually gifts in disguise, we will see that making that dreaded mistake is the right thing to do, and we will have nothing to feel bad about. Once we recognize that our mistakes give us opportunities to become greater than we knew we could be, coming face to face with our darkness will become freeing and empowering. This, then, is where Kabbalah departs completely from conventional views: From a kabbalistic perspective, darkness is actually the path to Light. By overcoming it, we reveal our true gifts. What a life-altering way to look at depression!

Of course, if one of the best ways to vanquish darkness and reveal Light is to transform our negative traits, we must first have some negative traits to begin with—something that most of us can manage! Next, we must identify these traits, and the most efficient and precise way to do so is by falling. When Sam fell behind in his homework, it allowed him to recognize—albeit painfully—that he had problems with time management and procrastination. Had he not fallen, he would have remained ignorant of his less desirable qualities and would have missed an opportunity to transform his negativity into Light. And had Sam chosen to remain engulfed by depression, he would have passed up a chance to reinvigorate his desire.

The lure of avoidance was tempting for Sam, as it is for all of us— especially those of us with depression, who often feel additionally weighted down by feelings of guilt and helplessness. We often find ourselves wondering why we should bother taking action at all, when sticking our heads in the proverbial sand would be so much easier for us to do. But that's exactly where our real power comes—from resisting the desire to shut down and curl up in a ball. It is by resisting that we create Light in our lives.

But do you feel as though it's a constant fight, an endless strug-gle, to *not* give in to the temptation to shut down? If so, there is a good reason for this: It's because you are fighting a force that is doing everything in its power to keep your desire to connect with joy and happiness at an absolute minimum. In Kabbalah, that force is called the Opponent, and the Opponent's sole pur-pose is to keep you living in darkness. What is the Opponent? It is your very own ego, and it aspires to keep you oblivious to its real agenda.

We'll talk more about the Opponent later on, but for now, all you need to know is this: Where there is desire and Light, the Opponent has a difficult time throwing a punch. Remember, we don't need to free ourselves from depression in order to find our desire; we need to increase our desire in order to clear away depression. Draw desire back into your life, and your depression will begin to dissipate. Darkness and light cannot coexist, so when you connect to the Light, depression is forced to take the high road out of town.

QUICK SYSTEM REBOOT: EXERCISE #1

When you picked up this book, you did so because you or someone you love suffers from depression. Congratulations on taking a proactive step toward recovery! If you are the one who is experiencing depression, let's take a moment to shed some light on your darkness. Remember that overcoming depression starts with one small step, and we can do this next one together.

Take out a pen and a piece of paper, if possible, and answer the following questions. As you do, you'll see that there is a great deal of healing power involved in the physical act of writing. That's because the moment you put paper to pen, you are taking an action, which begins the process of increasing desire. So let's get to it.

1. When did you first begin feeling depressed?

_____

_____

_____

_____

_____

2. What would you say is the cause of your depression?

_____

_____

_____

_____

_____

3. Do you feel as if you made a mistake or failed at a task?
   If so, describe your experience.

_____

_____

_____

_____

4. Did a personal experience reveal traits about yourself
   that you do not like? If so, describe those traits and
   why you believe they are negative.

_____

_____

_____

_____

_____

If answering these questions sounds too difficult or painful right
now, it may be because when we're in the darkness of depression,

we often find it hard to believe that we can actually make a difference in our own lives. All too often we're mired in the belief that there's something wrong with us, that we're somehow less than other people—less talented, less worthy, less funny, less beautiful, less confident. We feel we are not capable of taking even a minuscule step toward bringing more joy into our lives. Through the distorting lens of depression, our mistakes and negative traits appear insurmountable. In fact, we often perceive our misdeeds as so awful that we do not feel we merit forgiveness, and so we give up. What's the point of trying to do better, we say, when we've already messed everything up? But remember that these thoughts are just the machinations of your ego, and there is more than enough Light in this universe to overcome any doubt and shame you might feel. By opening yourself up to this possibility even for a moment, you will allow a bit of this all-loving Light into your life.

And don't forget—the more undesirable the baggage you feel you carry, the more opportunity you have to transform this negativity into joy. This might sound counterintuitive, but it's the truth. And happily, you don't have to take my word for it; just continue to use the technology of Kabbalah, and you will see for yourself. Once again, if you need help with this exercise or just need to talk, don't hesitate to call 1-800-KABBALAH and speak to a coach. And again, I encourage you to answer the above questions completely before reading on.

ADAM'S FALL

No one is immune to feeling depressed after a fall. The sacred text of Kabbalah known as *The Zohar* explains that Adam himself fell into this space. But the primary lesson to be learned from the story of Adam is not that Adam should have yielded to God's instruction, but rather that he should have seen the opportunity his momentary lapse in judgment revealed. Rav Ashlag, one of the greatest kabbalists of the 20th century, actually wrote in one of his essays that Adam and Eve *had* to fall in order to create the world in which we live.

So according to the kabbalists, Adam's fall was not a mistake at all; instead, falling was written into his DNA. Adam's real challenge lay in seizing the opportunity to move past his misdeed and rise to the occasion by righting his wrong. Put another way, Adam's fall was not a physical one but rather a fall in his consciousness. By failing to recognize his mistake as a chance to reveal Light, Adam forgot the purpose for which he had come into this world.

So when God called to Adam, "Where are you?" it wasn't that God literally couldn't find his own creation hiding behind a bush! Instead, God was questioning Adam's state of mind. God was asking Adam where he had gone within his own consciousness. Having disregarded God's wishes, Adam saw the gravity of his mistake and thought that he had blown it. *The Zohar*, which helps decode the Bible's hidden messages, explains that instead of seeing an opportunity to take responsibility for his actions, Adam withdrew further into himself. In fact, he spent the next 130 years bringing more negativity into the world and wallowing in his own shortcomings. We might say that Adam was the first person to suffer from depression and from the harsh self-judgments that it brings, which often cause us to withdraw not only from society but even from ourselves.

This type of self-incrimination shrinks our Vessel, thereby nearly extinguishing our desire. In depression, we fall into the trap of believing we have no right to desire joy, that we don't deserve happiness. What we often fail to understand is that harsh self-reproach disconnects us from the very happiness we crave. Each time we brush ourselves off after a fall *despite* our tendency to beat ourselves up, we bring ourselves one step closer to freedom from depression. I am not saying that this process is a cake-walk, but it is certain to be healing. From this point on, then, try to view your missteps, your screw-ups, your "less thans," and your falls not as justifications for self-punishment and emotional shut down but rather as opportunities for transformation and growth.

When students come to me seeking advice, I remind them that we were not created as angels but as human beings, with a built-in tendency to fall. As my mother always says, angels live in heaven; humans live on earth. We were meant to make mistakes and to recognize those mistakes for what they are and try something a bit different the next time around. My mother has also been known to ask rhetorically, "Why do you think pencils have erasers?" Mistakes are not only okay, but are an unavoidable part of the DNA of the physical world. So you might as well just accept the notion that we are all going to fall. But this doesn't mean we have to live in fear, shut ourselves off from the world, and disengage from life just to make sure we'll never screw up. On the contrary, we should embrace our inherent nature! For without mistakes, we would never grow.

Consider the mythical phoenix. Each time this incredible winged creature rises from his own ashes, he emerges that much more powerful. For him as well as for us, messing up is cause for celebration! By getting back on our feet, we align ourselves with our purpose on this planet while at the same time sparking the desire for change. And each time we connect with our desire, we apply the antidote to depression at its very root. The key is to not shut down or close ourselves off in an effort to protect our ego, but to face the consequences of our actions and grow from them.

PART TWO

THE POWER OF THE LIGHT

According to Kabbalah, life is meant to be filled with joyful Light. We are not here to suffer; we are here to be fulfilled. Connecting to the Light is the source of this fulfillment. But what is the Light? We talked about it earlier, but it's time to take a closer look. As you might remember, the Light is a powerful energy that exists within each of us as well as within every element on this planet, from rocks, to oak trees, to elephants, to the air we breathe. The power to heal ourselves lies not only within us but all around us as well. The Light is everywhere.

The Light is never-ending joy. It is unconditional love and compassion, both for ourselves and for others. It existed long before any of us were here; it's where we all came from and where we are all headed. Each of us has experienced it, if only briefly. Any moments in which we have felt genuinely happy, when bliss has washed over us—that positive state of fulfillment was a spark of the Light. The awe experienced with the birth of a child; the satisfaction of finishing a painting, a story, or a recipe; the exhilaration of finding common ground with a new friend or an old love; the pristine, mind-blowing beauty of a mountain range in the depth of winter; the comfort of a loved one nestled in a chair beside us; the source of all of these sparks of pleasure and fulfillment is the Light.

I am often asked to describe what it might feel like to live entirely within the Light—in other words, to have a constant connection and not just momentary sparks. If you can imagine, according to Kabbalah, living in this realm is 60 times more fulfilling than the greatest orgasm! Experiencing this constant state of satisfaction would require an immense capacity for fulfillment—or quite a Vessel, in kabbalistic terms. That is why we continually expand our Vessel and our desire to be able to hold that much fulfillment. In fact, it would take an infinitely large cup to hold all the divine goodness and fulfillment that is available and accessible to each of us.

If living entirely within the Light is divine goodness beyond our imagination, we all know what it is like to live apart from the Light. This way of living couldn't be further removed from ecstasy. In it, we feel unsure and precarious, as if the ground were shifting beneath us while we carry the weight of the world on our shoulders. We go through our lives being swayed one way by this external stimulus and another way by that one. No wonder we have such a difficult time finding our footing, much less any real peace!

Just as easily as external events can trigger happiness in our emotional psyche, they can also trigger sorrow. Death, famine, loss, failure—these things pull us away from happiness. Living within the Light means we are no longer at the mercy of events that are happening outside of us. But that doesn't mean we cut ourselves off from life. Not at all. In fact, it's really just a matter of changing the way we look at life, which serves to transform the level of consciousness at which we are living.

Living within the Light also means that we have ceased to see events and people in our lives as either "bad" or "good." What's the harm in doing this? Well, as soon as we define something in our lives as "bad," it becomes nearly impossible to view that person or event as the growth opportunity that it really represents.

Imagine that you are in graduate school working hard to earn your doctorate. You tell yourself that if you don't finish your dissertation and graduate in May, you will be a failure. In your mind, not graduating in May would be the worst outcome imaginable. So when May comes and goes and you still have work to complete, you become depressed and angry with yourself. What happened here is that you attached a specific meaning to graduating at a certain time. You equated graduating in May as the "right" time to graduate, maybe even the "only" time to graduate. Not graduating at this time would in your mind be "bad." Then, when you didn't meet the expectation you had set for yourself, by inference you became "bad" as well.

We do this to ourselves all the time, on a daily basis. We build elaborate scenarios in our minds based on arbitrary meanings we have assigned to various events. If this person compliments me, then it must mean that I'm worthy. If I complete this task, then it means I am a success. If I don't make an A, then I must be a failure. Do you see the black-and-white thinking that is at work here? But the Creator does not view life in terms of black and white, so why should we? Remember that the Light contains every shade of the rainbow. Yet when we get trapped in our black-and-white, "if-then" thinking, we allow ourselves to lose sight of the reality in which we live—one in which possibilities and potential abound.

The solution to this way of living lies in a total shift in the way we view the people and events that we encounter. What if instead of assigning meaning based on what we believe to be "good" or "bad," we viewed everything in our path as an opportunity, custom-designed to bring out our very best and to help us to reveal our true potential? When we perceive experiences in this way, our lives become richer, and events take on a much deeper meaning.

Not to mention, we are no longer attached to something outside of ourselves to define who we are. When we define ourselves on the basis of external events or things, our self-worth changes from one moment to the next. Perhaps in the morning we receive a promotion at work, and so we feel competent—but at lunch our boyfriend dumps us, so we feel unattractive, worthless, and unlovable. Then, that same evening, our best friend closes a deal on her new apartment, bringing back some of the morning's joy while also causing us to feel envious and worthless. But when we live with the Light on inside of us, we greet all occurrences with an equal sense of possibility. This means that "good" and "bad" events no longer exist as such. I am reminded of the Chinese tale of the farmer, his son, and the white horse. For those of you who are unfamiliar with this story, I will share it here.

> There was once a poor farmer who lived with his young son far from the main village. He and his son had only one horse to help them plow their fields. This horse was magnificent—so magnificent, in fact, that one day, when the emperor was passing through, he heard about the horse and offered the farmer a considerable sum of money to buy it. The farmer refused to sell the animal. That same night, the horse ran off.

> In the morning, the villagers flocked around the farmer saying, "Oh, how awful! What a bad thing has happened to you! You don't have your horse anymore, and you don't have the king's gold!"

> The farmer responded, "Maybe it is bad, maybe it is not. All I know is that my horse is gone and I don't have the emperor's gold."

Several days passed, and then one morning the magnificent white horse returned, bringing with him six other beautiful but wild horses, each one of which would be more valuable than the last once they were broken and trained.

Now the villagers gathered and said, "Oh, how wonderful! What a good thing has happened to you! You will soon be a very wealthy man!"

To which the farmer responded, "Maybe it is good, maybe it is not. All I know is that my horse has returned and brought six more horses with him."

Soon after the horse's return, the farmer's son was thrown from one of the wild horses, and both of his legs were broken in the fall.

Once more the villagers came, and this time they said, "Oh, what a tragedy has befallen you! You will never be able to break these horses by yourself, and now you have no one to help you with your crops, which will cause you to suffer great losses and perhaps go hungry."

The farmer said, "Maybe it is bad, maybe it is not. All I know is that my son was thrown from a horse and has broken both his legs."

The next day the emperor returned to the village. This time he was leading his soldiers to a brutal battle with a neighboring country and was rounding up new recruits, most of whom would be marching to certain death. Because of his injuries, the farmer's son was passed over.

This time the villagers, who were full of grief at the loss of their own sons, rushed to the farmer and exclaimed, "Your son has been spared! You are blessed! It was a good thing that he fell off the horse and broke both his legs. Now he will not die like the rest of the boys from the village."

And the farmer replied, "Maybe it is bad, maybe it is not. All I know is that my son did not have to join the emperor in his fight."

Although the story ends here, it is easy enough to imagine the farmer's life continuing in the same manner. By treating all external events equally and by not adding meaning to each twist and turn that life brings, the farmer keeps his Vessel open to receive Light. In contrast, the townspeople continue to allow each occurrence to sway their emotions like a tree branch in a fierce storm. If we behave like the townspeople in this story, we risk expending precious energy searching for a "good" thing or seeking something to counteract a "bad" experience. It is this constant quest for external highs, which by their very nature are impermanent and therefore ultimately unsatisfying, that causes the lows that we feel.

Consider economics. Let's say that every time we experienced an economic depression, the government decided to print a whole bunch of new money and pass it out to everyone who needed it. What would happen? At first everyone would be thrilled, because they would now have money to spend when a moment before they were broke. But then what? With all of this new money floating around without a strong economy to back it up, the cost of goods and services would skyrocket. Where would that leave everyone? Worse off than before. Why? Because now the same goods and services would be costlier than ever, making the true value of money lower than before. That's what happens when we use artificial methods to improve our economy—or our state of mind. In both cases, we create a temporary, artificial high that eventually causes us to crash. On the other hand, when we go through life without judging events as positive or negative and merely experience them exactly as they are, we eliminate the need for imitation highs or emotional inflation. And instead, we get the real deal—a joyful, blessed, Light-filled existence.

Shifting our perspective in this way also gives us the ability to recognize that everything that happens to us—even the "bad"—is actually an opportunity for "good." So when we lose our job, get dumped over dinner, or crash the car, rather than experiencing these events as failures, we can begin to see them as no different from finding a new job. In fact, we learn that these events can provide us with an even greater chance to connect with the Light, so long as we are able to view them as opportunities for spiritual growth.

Let me share another story with you to illustrate this point. Elizabeth began attending talks at one of our Kabbalah Centres many years ago. She was in her mid-40s at the time and had worked hard to address the depression with which she had struggled throughout her life. I met her at a time when she felt her life was going well and was seeking to delve a bit deeper into the spiritual meaning of her existence. After several months of study and increased confidence regarding the direction her life was taking, Elizabeth unexpectedly lost her job. Having seen no warning signs, she experienced this as quite a blow. In fact, she had been feeling so secure in her position that she had begun to make arrangements to purchase a new home. The news sent Elizabeth into a familiar spiral of doubt and fear. She felt that she was a failure because she had lost her job, and her mind compounded the loss even further: Now she would never be able to purchase a home, would never find another job in her field, and would likely be forced to move in with her parents while everyone around her remained happy and successful. All her recent progress began to slip away into depression.

We had many long talks at the time, during which I encouraged Elizabeth to view her job loss as a neutral event in her life. It was neither good nor bad; it simply was. We also discussed some of the actions that may have led to her losing her position. It turned out that she had not been as proactive as she could have been and had failed to keep track of some accounts as carefully as her boss would have liked. At first, Elizabeth had a difficult time acknowledging her own role in her dismissal. But I continued to encourage her to view it through a nonjudgmental lens, and even to celebrate the discovery of her faults. Only then could she begin to transform them!

After several restless days, Elizabeth began to stop spiraling downward. "It's not good; it's not bad," she would repeat to herself. "I am simply no longer in the employ of that company."

With each repetition, she began to experience a sense of calm. Eventually Elizabeth's job came to an end, and she didn't find a new position right away. But in her free time, she began frequenting the local library with the goal of researching an idea she had for a company of her own. It was there that she met Alyssa, with whom she became fast friends, and through Alyssa she met Ralph, who later became her husband. Eventually Elizabeth also found well-paying and interesting employment. And she began to see her life the way the Chinese farmer saw his: as consisting solely of the present moment. Her job, her marriage, and her friendships were neither good nor bad. They were simply opportunities to move toward the Light.

Like Elizabeth, we try our darnedest to avoid mistakes and failure in the hopes that by doing so, we'll bring joy into our lives. We live in constant fear that we'll be "found out," and that our negative traits will rise to the surface like cream in a churn. But one of the most exciting things I want to share with you is this: Even if a person came into this world and did absolutely everything right and never failed, he or she would be no closer to his or her true purpose in life.

Nor would this person have any more Light or fulfillment in comparison to another. Why? Because we come into this world in order to make mistakes and, through our mess-ups, to discover and transform our less desirable traits. By transforming our negative traits into qualities that are rooted in the act of sharing, we reveal beautiful Light. So if we were to do everything right in life, we wouldn't really be doing anything at all. We would miss the whole point of our messed-up existence, because we would not have revealed any Light.

Remember the Opponent that I mentioned earlier? One of the Opponent's best strategies is to induce us to hate ourselves when we see our faults rather than to rejoice in them. There is a tool I'd like to share with you that is meant to counteract this impulse. What would happen if you simply observed your negative trait rather than reacting to it in disgust? Try simply being an observer instead of someone who is emotionally invested in the outcome. Withhold judgment while you stand on the sidelines, and watch how that quality plays out. Note how the trait has undermined your existence and interfered with your goals and expectations. But don't judge; just observe. In this way, you will be acting like the Creator, who does not judge but instead loves unconditionally.

Often, after people have tried this exercise, they come to me hating themselves even more and wondering how they should go about fixing the trait that they have so diligently observed. No one likes to see their shortcomings at first, but there is no need for us to expend energy trying to fix them. Why? Because according to Rav Ashlag, it is our nature to rebel against that which is revolting to us. After having observed our trait in action over time and having witnessed its effect on our lives, we will naturally turn away from it. Furthermore, if we allow ourselves to experience the discomfort that this trait has caused us and allow our very essence to become repulsed by it, we will begin to transform naturally. It is against our nature to keep putting our hand into a fire that is scalding us. We will pull our hand away instinctively once we feel the pain.

The fire, in this case, is the negative trait. When you come to understand that putting your hand in this fire will burn and hurt you, you will eventually stop doing so, right? The problem is that our negative tendencies often cause us only indirect pain, so we don't always perceive a direct connection between the two. Certainly it would be great to know that THIS ACTION = THIS PAIN, but we are rarely given such a straightforward equation with which to work. But by patiently observing a negative tendency and witnessing its consequences over time, we will instinctively and naturally move our hand away from the flame.

Think of your negative quality as a smudge of dirt or a dust bunny lying in the corner of your living room. If we avoid this piece of dirt or hide it away in shame, it will never be removed. But if we shine a light on it and focus our attention on it, we will be able to see precisely where it is—under the couch, on the window, or in the corner. It will then start to bother us until we finally grab a cloth and gently wipe it away.

Any negative trait that we might possess—our garbage, if you will—is no different from this smudge of dirt. When we shine the Light on our garbage, we can see it for what it truly is and what it truly does, and only then can we start to clean it up. For example, we will start catching the negative words we use when we speak to our loved ones or the hateful tapes we play in our heads, and we will naturally try a different approach. Why? Because we know by now that we won't get the results we seek by choosing the same path we have always taken. But if we have no awareness of how our garbage plays out, then we will never be inclined to change our current modus operandi, and our garbage will continue to control us.

When we judge our negative qualities and stash them away in shame, what we are really doing is keeping ourselves in the dark. That's because by denying our negative traits, we disconnect ourselves from the blessings that life intends for us. But when we transform a negative trait into Light, we swing open a massive gate that allows blessings from the universe to envelop us. So our real work involves allowing ourselves to view our traits from the perspective of a bystander, *without bias*. This step alone opens the window through which Light can enter and begin to transform our harmful traits into radiance.

A DISCONNECT

Depression, in kabbalistic terms, means that we have disconnected from the Light. All of us, whether or not we are consciously aware of it, are trying in one way or another to rediscover our connection to the Light; this is our purpose on earth. Depression is simply one of the many ways in which we can lose our footing, and, as such, it is no different from struggling with alcoholism, anger, excessive spending, or a lack of self-esteem. No issue is better or worse than any other; they all weaken or sever our connection with the Light.

A severed connection from the Light means that we cut ourselves off from pleasure, excitement, and euphoria. The Light is so vibrant, uplifting, and restorative that its loss can have devastating effects. Some of us seek to fill the emptiness with drugs, sex, or material possessions, but at best, all of these stimuli produce only fleeting imitations of joy, after which the darkness inevitably returns. For those of us who are struggling with depression, the darkness can be misleading. It can feel familiar, and even like a refuge from pain. The Opponent wouldn't have it any other way. But there is an alternative to this well-worn path.

When darkness beckons, instead of allowing it to envelop us, we can recognize it as a gentle cue to seek opportunities that produce Light. More specifically, the approaching darkness can serve as a reminder that it's time for us to reach out and share our gifts with others who are struggling even more than we are. And trust me, you do have gifts—that I can promise you. And by the time you finish this book, you won't need my assurances to know this at the very core of your being. So bid the looming darkness farewell as you take a moment to smile at a homeless woman on the street or pick up the phone to call a friend who needs your support. Impulses such as these are invitations to embrace the Light.

Another way to counteract an episode of depression is to look for the beauty in the moment. For example, suppose a mother who feels burdened and depressed snaps at her child when he asks for a cup of juice. The mother's depression is now compounded by the wrong she feels she did to her child by snapping at him. From there, our tendency is to spiral deeper into the darkness. But what if we turned this cycle around? What if the mother knelt down and offered her son a sincere apology for her actions? In response, the child smiles and acknowledges his mother's gesture. Who could fail to see the love and sincerity of this moment? The potential for beauty and Light exists in every moment—especially those that seem ugly and uncomfortable at first glance.

One of the keys to realizing the potential for beauty lies in recognizing that there is a force that wants us to overlook these special moments completely. This force—the Opponent—would prefer that we see only the negative side of a situation rather than looking beyond it to find the good. In the previous example, the Opponent imbues the mother with a sense of shame, thereby making it hard for her to admit to her child that she has reacted poorly. But if the mother is able to acknowledge her lapse, she can seize a priceless opportunity to teach her child that it is okay to be wrong—that it is okay to make mistakes.

When we fight negative forces such as shame, we connect to the Light, allowing ourselves to enjoy the moment at hand. Instead of automatically responding to a moment in the same ineffective way we have in the past, we acknowledge the Opponent's influence and refrain from reacting to it. This opens our Vessel to receive Light, thereby giving us the power to turn any moment into a divinely inspired event as well as an opportunity for genuine connection and growth.

When we are struggling with depression, it is helpful to remember past moments we have experienced that have embodied Light. A moment of creative inspiration; a time when we truly helped another human being; a split second during which we saw the bigger picture of life; a profound connection while making love; the contemplation of a snowflake on a window pane or nose; forgetting about our troubles entirely while playing with a puppy; hugging a dear friend we haven't seen in quite some time—all are examples of connecting with the Light. And if you've made that connection once, then you can do it again and again.

Before we move on, I'd like to point out one of the common mistakes we all make, which is to confuse a person or thing with the Light. Amid the euphoria of falling in love, for example, we often tend to associate our beloved one with intense feelings of happiness, and we therefore equate the object of our love with the source of our joy. Faced with the departure of this person, we fear that our well-being is threatened. While it is true that our partner is also composed of Light, this person can no more siphon off his or her Light and give it to us, than we can give him or her our ability to speak Mandarin Chinese or play guitar. In other words, our beloved is not the true source of our happiness. We may revel in our time together, but it is our interaction with the other person—not the individual per se—that makes us happy. It is our ability to care, to be present, and to share with another that opens the door to Light. When we lose that desire to go outside of ourselves and be fully present for another, we start to fall into our old patterns of insecurity and fear. And when we fall to this level of consciousness, we lose our lifeline to the source of all things good.

QUICK SYSTEM REBOOT: EXERCISE #2

Let's pause here and think about a time or times when you knew that you were experiencing the Light. I mentioned a few examples, but I know that you have some moments of your own that you could list in the space below. When you're in the fog of depression, it may seem as if I'm asking you to pull a rabbit out of a hat. But really I'm not. You just have to think for a moment. Take a deep breath and ask the Light to reveal these moments to you. After you have done this, take a second to write down a joyful time that comes to mind.

_____

_____

_____

_____

_____

_____

_____

_____

_____

_____

_____

_____

REBOOTING

The more we work together to lift the fog of depression by connecting to the Light, the more aware you will become of the joy
that surrounds you. Pausing to reflect on delightful moments
that you have been a part of helps cultivate a sense of gratitude
for the good in your life. I encourage you to use this tool frequently. And once again, please make it a priority to finish this
exercise before moving on to the next chapter.

PART THREE

OUR TWO
REALITIES

REBOOTING

If you were told that you could enter a room flooded with warm, radiant Light that made you feel wholly loved and at total peace or, alternatively, a room that held nothing but suffocating darkness, which would you choose? Of course, you'd choose to enter the room that emitted loving Light. But my question isn't really hypothetical, for the choice is yours every day, one small decision at a time.

When we choose to live a Light-filled existence, we are choosing to live in what kabbalists call the 99% Realm. However, when we choose to exist in darkness and depression, we are choosing the 1% Realm. These two realms exist simultaneously, and it is our choices and actions that determine which one we will live in. In our practical day-to-day lives, we live in both. If we suffer from depression, we live mostly in the 1% Realm. As you will soon discover, our work as human beings can bring the realm of the 99% both to ourselves and to the rest of world. We can learn to shed light on the shadowy nooks and crannies of our inner lives—and beyond.

The 1% Realm is the one with which we are more familiar, and the one to which we commonly refer when we use words such as *fleeting, impermanent,* or *external.* We have spent most of our lives in the 1% Realm, as have the majority of the people we know, although we're probably not aware of it. This is the physical realm, that of the emotions and of the five senses. It's called the 1% Realm because ancient kabbalists, as well as modern physicists, tell us that 1% or less of our vast universe is actual physical matter and the other 99% is energy. For example, when we see an object such as a table, we assume that what we are seeing is completely solid, but it's not. In actuality, the amount of matter that makes up the table is infinitesimal, while the energy fields that surround each tiny particle of matter are vast. So a table is mostly vibrating, pulsating energy that takes on the illusion of physicality.

To illustrate this idea further, let's use a well-known monument, the Eiffel Tower. Physicists say that the amount of actual physical matter in the Eiffel Tower would fill nothing larger than a matchbox. A matchbox! The remainder of what we see and experience from this immense structure consists of energy.

Everything in the 1% Realm suffers from entropy—the second law of thermodynamics—in that each ounce of material in the physical world of the 1% comes to an end. Someone builds a skyscraper; wind, rain, and sleet wear against its façade; and eventually it begins to fall apart. We are born, we grow up, we grow old, perhaps we become ill, and then we die. There is no possibility of the infinite in the 1% Realm. Nothing that exists purely as a physical entity can resist the effects of time.

The 1% Realm is also the realm of reaction and, by extension, chaos. When we are connected to the 1% Realm, we are connected to our own reactive nature. According to Kabbalah, our reactive nature is the cause of all of our suffering. How is this the case? When we fail to pause before reacting to a situation, we not only create chaos in that moment but also cause chaos to boomerang back into our lives at a later time. It's like pushing the first domino in a line of many: Once the first domino has fallen, you can't take it back. The chaos of the 1% Realm begets more chaos until we learn to resist our reactive nature. In Part Five we'll discuss specific ways to resist reactive behavior, and expanding our Vessel to receive Light.

INSTANT GRATIFICATION

Despite the fact that the 1% Realm is one of chaos, we can't deny that this realm offers a host of instant pleasures. Let's be honest; we wouldn't remain trapped in this realm if we perceived it as pure pain. Even when we are depressed, we can remember moments of pleasure, even if we temporarily cannot experience them as such: late-night movies, road trips with best friends, home-cooked meals, falling in love, gardening, solving a problem, building a dream home, the list goes on and on. Yes, these are pleasurable things. But the point here is this: Be careful not to confuse momentary pleasure with genuine joy.

Joy is substantial and lasting, whereas pleasure, by its very nature, is impermanent. Try to think of one instance in which a pleasurable situation has endured in its pristine, original form. It's impossible, isn't it? The warmth of the summer sun eventually produces sweat, headaches, and sunburn. The big job we're so proud of changes when a new boss steps in or when our interests shift direction. Innocent infatuation gives way to frustration when one of the two parties fails to invest the emotion and caring required to achieve lasting love. Even sex becomes monotonous and tiresome if the connection is only physical. It is good to experience the pleasures of the 1%

Realm, and it is good to get satisfaction from them, but don't forget that those pleasures are fleeting. They are inherently incapable of bringing us lasting happiness or relief from depression. If we seek remedies for depression in the 1% Realm alone, we will only find ways to cope with our depression, but we will not find the means to conquer it.

That's because . . .

When we focus on and live in the 1% Realm, we are in affinity with a dimension that has no Light of its own.

The 1% Realm, from a kabbalistic perspective, is referred to as *Malchut*, which is the Vessel of the Light. The kabbalists explain that the realm of *Malchut* corresponds to the moon because *Malchut*, like the moon, emits no light of its own. The only reason it appears to glow in the sky is that it reflects the light of the sun. In other words, the 1% Realm is merely darkness disguised as radiance. The sun is the true source of light. According to Kabbalah, the sun, also known as *Zeir Anpin*, corresponds to the 99%. And the 99%, like the sun, is infinite Light. Only when we connect to this realm of lasting Light can we find a true cure for our depression.

But the catch is this: The infinite, blissful Light of the 99% Realm is largely concealed from our five senses, so we often forget that it is even there—until we experience it. According to *The Zohar*, the 99% Realm is called the Endless because it contains never-ending happiness and joy—not the types of happiness and joy that come and go, but happiness and joy that abide. In the 99% Realm, our desires are instantly and constantly fulfilled. If the 1% Realm is the realm of pleasure, then the 99% Realm is the realm of lasting fulfillment.

We experience the Light of the 99% not by attempting to satisfy our external needs, but by working to reveal the Light that exists within us. Remember, we each have the means to access this Light. This realm does not lie beyond our grasp, nor is it something dreams are made of. It's very real—just as real as the chair or couch you are sitting on or the book that you are reading.

But all too often we confuse the tangible with the real—accepting as fact only that which we can physically touch, see, hear, taste, or smell. We make the mistake of dismissing energetic realities as metaphorical at best, or inventions of unstable minds at worst. But all the major religions and an ever-expanding segment of the scientific world recognize both matter *and* energy as real. As we've already discussed, nothing in the 1% Realm lasts. Even those things we may take for granted, such as the soundness of our bodies and our minds, will eventually evolve and change. When something we particularly enjoy or depend on doesn't last—we lose our health, a close friend moves away, our child goes off to college, a beloved pet dies— we typically react to the change by seeing everything as perishable and becoming depressed. What we are lacking in these moments is an awareness of the 99% Realm, an awareness of the Realm of the Light that is present in each of us and does not end.

Some very wise people have walked the earth encouraging people to develop an awareness of the loving Light that burns inside us all. Not long ago, the Gospels of Thomas were discovered in a jar buried in Egypt. These gospels portray Jesus as a teacher who speaks in parables and asks his followers to look for the kingdom of God not in heaven, but within themselves. At one point Jesus says to his followers, "When you come to dwell in the Light, what will you do? On the day when you were one you became two. But when you become two, what will you do?" Jesus is referring to the existence of the Light and our separation from it, and he is asking us, How, then, will we connect to it again? Later, Jesus tells his followers, "If you bring forth what is within you, what you have will save you." He is once more referring to the Light, that spark of the Creator that is within us all.

Our job as human beings is to unite the 1% Realm and the 99% Realm by bringing this Light to the physical world in which we live. Only human beings have access to both realities, which means that only human beings may experience the true totality of existence—the entire sum of both worlds.

We learn to bring Light into our physical world by using the various tools and exercises that we describe in this book. They help us connect to the 99% Realm, expand our Vessel, and harness the infinite Light that is ours for the taking. There is only one surefire way to remove our depression—and that is to expand our Vessel so that Light can pour in and fill all the emotional cracks and fissures that lead us to feel fragile and empty.

QUICK SYSTEM REBOOT: EXERCISE #3

Think of a situation that you are currently experiencing that seems rooted in the 1% Realm. Perhaps you are experiencing chaos in a close relationship, or someone near to you has a chronic illness and is suffering. The situation feels dark and heavy. Describe it in the space provided:

_____

_____

_____

_____

_____

_____

_____

_____

_____

_____

Now pause for a moment. How could you expand your Vessel in this situation and bring Light into the picture? If you are feeling resistance right now, that's understandable. When our Vessel is small and our desire close to nil, we can't help but feel a little hopeless. All I'm asking is that you take the darkness that you are feeling and expose it to just a little Light. Think about it, and please don't read another sentence until you have written down one small action that you can take to bring the Light of the 99% into your physical world.

_____

_____

_____

_____

_____

_____

_____

_____

_____

_____

_____

_____

THE OPPONENT: OPEN ALL DAY, EVERY DAY

REBOOTING

If the 99% Realm is open to us and the Light is bountiful and healing, you may be wondering, why do we cut ourselves off from it? As you might recall, it is the Opponent that encourages us to disconnect. According to Kabbalah, this force was created in order to provide us with the opportunity to overcome our obstacles and experience true joy. As hard as it might be to believe, the Opponent plays a vital role in our ability to reveal Light.

The Opponent, also known as Satan (pronounced suh-tan), is not some pitchfork-wielding goblin dressed in red tights and a leotard. Rather, Satan, the Opponent, is our ego. All of us have an ego—even the most humble of humans. We are accustomed to thinking of people with egos as insufferable jerks who can't stop talking about their Botox injections or how well they play golf. But people who suffer from low self-esteem, shyness, and feelings of inferiority have egos as well. In both cases—whether the person comes across as overbearing or self-deprecating—the ego is playing a highly influential role.

That's because the ego has a very persuasive voice. And that voice seems to become all the more persuasive in the face of depression. For instance, that budding idea you had about volunteering at the local community center, going to the gym, or cleaning your apartment is often overshadowed by the ego's sense that it's just not worth the effort. Thoughts that might confirm that you are capable, smart, funny, talented, and not alone can't seem to gain a strong foothold either. And that feeling that your life is filled with blessings and joy is nipped in the bud before it has a chance to bloom. Your ego is responsible for all of these abortive attempts at finding joy. And just so you know . . .

Your ego is constantly engaged. It doesn't need to sleep, or eat, or use the bathroom. It never shuts up.

So why does the Creator allow the Opponent to exist? Consider history, mythology, and literature. Heroes and happy endings could not exist without a worthy adversary. Would Harry Potter have attained such high levels of inner personal growth without Voldemort there to thwart his every step? Or consider computer games. Your animated hero jumps levels only by defeating a foe who puts up a worthy fight. And for every level your hero rises, his enemy becomes increasingly powerful. The stronger the Opponent, the more glory your hero—that is, your true soul—stands to gain. In other words, the tougher and more difficult the obstacles, the greater the Light there is to be revealed. Do you ever wonder where these universal truths come from? No matter what our culture, religion, age, or level of education, we all understand innately that the greater the challenge, the greater the reward. The hero's journey is just humanity's life story.

That is why the bottom line of our nature is this:

Everyone wants to achieve his or her greatest potential.

This is a universal truth no matter what issues we may be struggling with. Those suffering from anxiety want to achieve their greatest potential, as do people with anger issues, abandonment issues, phobias, and depression. And it's the Opponent who gives us the opportunity to reach our greatest potential. Without the Opponent, there would be no circumstances for us to overcome, no difficulties for us to creatively solve, no failures from which we could grow and mature spiritually. Thus, it doesn't matter if the Opponent shows up as a fire-breathing dragon or as the internal demons of our negative thoughts, hell-bent on keeping us mixed up or feeling down. Regardless of the circumstance, the battle is one for our own greatness.

Although the Opponent gives us opportunities for growth, he would prefer that we didn't see them as such. Instead, he would prefer to see us stumble at each twist and turn without brushing ourselves off and standing back up. That's because the Opponent's job is to distract us from reaching our highest potential. And he accomplishes this by keeping us caught up in our depression rather than dedicating ourselves to achieving our divine potential. Remember, depression is not the primary issue we face. Certainly when we are in the thick of it, it may feel that way. But depression is the effect of one true cause: lack of desire. And the Opponent has myriad tools with which to keep us sidetracked from the real work at hand: reigniting this desire. He tries relentlessly to convince us that we shouldn't bother to want what we cannot possibly have. He tells us that things will always be this way—that we will never make it; we will never change. These are the words the Opponent uses to keep our desires dormant. He has convinced us that we should not want anything—that it's not worth it. It is simply not worth the fight.

ME, ME, ME

One of the ego's techniques for keeping our Vessel small and the desire in our lives at a minimum is to keep us constantly focused on ourselves. No one else matters in the world of the ego. For this reason, the ego incites us to believe that other people's actions and responses have everything to do with us. In other words, the ego wants us to take everything personally. For instance, we might mistake a friend's quest for happiness as a deliberate attempt to make us feel bad. But why would someone—especially a friend—set out to make us feel miserable? As crazy as it may sound, the ego can influence just about anyone to travel this negative road. In a similar manner, how often have you thought that a friend, a lover, or a boss was ignoring you or being rude to you or was even out to get you, only to find that they had suffered a personal tragedy or were preoccupied with an important project? Only then did you realize that it was not about you. They weren't withdrawing from you, but from everybody.

The Opponent *wants* us to feel slighted. He *encourages* us to feel wronged because this requires energy from us—energy that we might otherwise use to get closer to the Light. In this way, our egocentric behavior feeds our depression. And the more depressed we become, the stronger the Opponent will be.

And just as eagerly as we are led to feel slighted, our ego will lap up any compliment that comes our way. This is because compliments temporarily inflate our sense of self—the key word here being *temporary*. Someone likes our new car, and our ego beams; someone else thinks our business plan is brilliant, and our ego turns cartwheels; the guitar riff we wrote makes our neighbor weep with joy, and our ego throws a party. The ego wants us to be addicted to compliments and external approval rather than thriving on the lasting satisfaction that can be found in our own efforts and transformation—the lasting satisfaction that comes from discovering our own Light.

When we find ourselves taking the actions of other people personally, be it flattery or abuse, this is our ego speaking, telling us that we are the center of the universe—that everything that happens in our lives revolves around us. This focus on self alone separates us from the Light. It is only when we resist our self-seeking, reactive nature and are present for others that we sync up with the joy that the Creator intended for us. We'll talk more about becoming present later in this chapter.

HAPPENING TO OURSELVES

The Opponent is cunning, to say the least. He loves to use time as a means of making life appear random and chaotic. He tricks us into thinking that things happen suddenly and unpredictably. Let's explore this misconception more carefully, because reversing such thinking is fundamental to overcoming depression.

So many of us—including those of us with depression—believe that much if not all of life happens *to* us, often suddenly and without rhyme or reason. How frequently have you used the word *suddenly*? Suddenly he quit his job. Suddenly she broke up with him. They suddenly moved to Idaho. But how sudden is sudden? For instance, have you ever awakened one morning to find that your home has suddenly doubled in size? Or that a tree has suddenly grown outside your window? Or that your children are suddenly in high school? Most likely not. Suddenness implies chaos, and chaos is an aspect of the 1% Realm, remember?

Chaos implies that things happen to us. But the reality is this:

Things don't happen to us; we happen to ourselves.

This means that we shape our own lives. We choose the way in which we view our world. Furthermore, we choose how quickly or slowly we want to work on changing, and how much effort we want to dedicate to increasing our level of desire. In fact, every single aspect of our lives and all the associated pleasures and pains are something we ourselves have generated, even if we have done so inadvertently. Kabbalah teaches us that things *don't* just happen to us, and that we are *not* merely arbitrary victims of chaos.

So what does that really mean? It means that our own actions and reactions are pivotal to a joyful, depression-free existence. More specifically, the action of standing up after we fall, instead of shutting down, is essential to dissolving our darkness. By owning up to all of our reactive thoughts, words, and actions and by growing because of them rather than denying their existence, we can literally remap our lives. That's because when we experience external events as happening to us, we lock ourselves into the 1% Realm, where chaos flourishes. But if we are happening to ourselves, we are connecting with the cause realm, or the 99%. By being proactive—by being the cause of our lives—we gain access to infinite possibilities. Perhaps unwittingly, we have already shaped our past. The incredible news is that we also have the power to shape our present and our future—and now we can do so more thoughtfully. Talk about empowering!

But remember that the Opponent wants to squelch this sense of empowerment and promote chaos instead. By using the powerful tool of time, the Opponent separates cause from effect so that we will easily lose sight of the consequences of our actions, thereby making life appear random and disjointed. The Opponent encourages us to believe that because an event occurred in the past and its effect is taking place in the present, the two events are not connected. A negative consequence can thus seem to be a "sudden" and random event. This time lag can make it appear as though good deeds go unrewarded and bad deeds go unpunished, when in fact nothing could be further from the truth. Perhaps it might take days, weeks, months, decades, or even lifetimes, but actions inevitably have consequences, and causes invariably have effects. Every seed we plant—whether it is inspired by the Light or by the Opponent—is guaranteed to show itself again at some point in the future as a tree in our backyard.

Let's use the environmental concerns of today as an example. It wasn't long ago that companies poured their toxic waste into oceans and rivers. Their belief was that our water supply was limitless and that no ill effects would result from such actions. Decades later, however, people from some waterfront towns began to develop diseases that were directly traceable to toxins. For better or for worse, the manner in which humans choose to interact with the earth's natural resources serves as a perfect example of cause and effect. Sometimes those effects may take decades or centuries to take hold, but they always do.

THE IMPORTANCE OF NOW

Remember that time is really just an illusion that the Opponent uses to confuse us. There is only one true moment—now. Now is really where the past, present, and future intersect. Confused? Let me clarify this point. In the now, we are living the effects of the seeds we have planted in the past. Our responses to those seeds bring about the circumstances we will encounter in our future. In other words, the now is the connective tissue that holds the past, present, and future together. This means that when we learn to stay in the now, we can correct the seeds of the past and plant positive and blessed seeds of fulfillment for the future.

So how we choose to experience and participate in this moment determines the opportunities we will receive in later moments. If we only partially invest our energy into a moment, we'll reap just a portion of what that moment had to offer. But when we view our awareness of each moment as an investment in the future, we become more attentive to our present surroundings.

Easy to understand but hard to do really. In fact, try it right now—try to stay present for five minutes without your mind wandering.

Challenging, isn't it? That's because the Opponent uses thoughts of the past and the future to distract us from being fully present. The Opponent gains the upper hand whenever we remain stuck in the past, fretting over something that was said or reliving a special moment, as well as when we become pre-occupied with the future, either by fantasizing about it or by feeling anxious over it. The truth is that our present captures a surprisingly small amount of our attention. And when we busy our minds with the past and the future, we become oblivious to the kinds of seeds we are planting in the here and now. The result? We unwittingly plant seeds of chaos into our lives.

The more we can ground ourselves in the present—even when the present is unpleasant—the stronger we will become and the weaker the Opponent will be. Take a moment now to observe the sounds around you. Feel the earth beneath your feet, or the cushion you are seated on. Watch how your mind reacts to this process. Does it calm, or does it speed up? How about your breathing? Remember that there is no right or wrong here; you are merely experiencing the present. Try to do this several times a day, perhaps before each meal, or upon rising and again before bed. Work up to longer periods of awareness. The Opponent knows that if you are in three places at once, your energy will begin to leak from your Vessel. But if you are in one place—if you are in the present—you will begin to take control of your energy rather than giving it away to the Opponent.

One way to practice being present is through meditation. Rather than seeing your daily activities as tasks to be checked off a list, you can imbue the act of washing the dishes, for example, or waiting in line at the store, with a heightened sense of awareness. When past recollections or future worries arise, recognize that they are there, and then nudge your focus back to the task at hand. Feel the warm water against your skin, listen to the drone of the faucet, smell the detergent, and watch the food scraps swirl down the drain. Focusing on your breath can be tremendously grounding as you experiment in this way. If you find your mind wandering, breathe deeply. Inhale for four counts, hold for four counts, and exhale for four counts. Do this until you feel you've regained your presence in the now. Even if you are able to hold the now for only a second, that's fantastic! That's one more second than you had before.

Practicing this exercise has an added benefit: It puts you in the best frame of mind for conquering the Opponent. When you learn to be more cognizant of the present, you can catch yourself when the Opponent sends difficult situations or thoughts your way. Instead of reacting without due process, you can assess the situation mindfully and respond in a manner that connects you with the 99% Realm. In addition, when we are consciously aware of our present, we are more likely to notice the needs of others and find ways to reach out and help make a difference. Thoughts of sharing come more naturally when we are grounded in the present.

Many people come to me complaining that their thoughts are always racing, making it nearly impossible for them to stay focused on the tasks and people at hand—no matter how important they might be. If you find yourself losing focus when you are talking with someone over the phone or in person, recognize this as an opportunity for you to bring Light into your world and the world of the person to whom you are talking. Losing focus serves as a gentle reminder that it's time to make an extra effort to truly connect with the person on the other end of the conversation. One of the teachers at The Kabbalah Centre says that when she finds her thoughts drifting but then makes a concerted effort to shift her focus to the other person, it awakens a psychic connection within her. That psychic connection is Light being revealed. The person can be thousands of miles away, but when she is able to direct her thoughts toward that person and share her undivided love and attention, she is directly connecting to the 99% Realm. We all have the power to manifest this divine connection. These seeds, which are inspired by the 99%, are the only seeds worth planting.

MISSED OPPORTUNITY

When we fail to connect to the now, we miss priceless opportunities for spiritual growth. This reminds me of a story about a young sage who lived many centuries ago. When this sage was in his 20's, he had a dream that a woman in need would one day come to him and ask for his assistance. In this dream, the man failed to give the woman the assistance she needed. He then searched and searched for her in order to reconcile his mistake, but to no avail. When the young sage awakened from his dream, he was filled with anxiety. His teacher cautioned him that this could be a signal to prepare him for the moment for which he came into this world. With that, he made a solemn commitment to seize the opportunity when it came to him in this lifetime.

A year passed, and the opportunity did not present itself despite the fact that the young sage had become dedicated to finding this woman. Ten years went by, and the sage was still actively seeking this opportunity. After twenty years his urgency began to fade, but the dream still lingered. Thirty years passed and then forty, until finally the sage forgot his dream completely.

PART FOUR: THE OPPONENT: OPEN ALL DAY, EVERY DAY   101

At the age of 65, on a cold and hectic day when there was more to do than the hours of the clock would allow, a small, quiet woman approached the sage. In a weak voice, she asked if the sage could please answer one question regarding her grandson. But by this time the sage had forgotten the dream and the opportunity, so he politely brushed the woman off and went about his affairs. After all, there were so many important tasks to complete! It was not until late that night, when he was sound asleep, that the dream came back to him. He woke up with full knowledge of the opportunity that he had missed—one for which he had waited his entire life.

He searched the entire town until he found the woman's humble home and knocked on the door. The woman opened the door slowly, and before she could even greet the sage, he apologized with the greatest degree of humility. He begged her for the opportunity to help and was relieved when she greeted him warmly and asked him to enter. Now the sage would finally fulfill his life's purpose.

The truth is that few of us know why we came into this world. It is only when we are present in the moment that we make ourselves accessible to life-changing opportunities that may present themselves to us at any given time. We must always be ready for such an occasion!

FINDING COMFORT IN THE NOW

When we allow ourselves to be fully present in the now, we realize that we are okay in this moment. And in the next. And the next. And the more moments of now we can string together, the more those voices of negativity subside. The Opponent has conditioned us to worry by viewing everything through the lens of the past or through the demands of the future. An afternoon spent in a lovely, safe apartment baking cookies is quite different from one spent in an apartment where you are not sure you can pay next month's rent or are stewing about having recently broken up with your girlfriend. The rent may be due and your girlfriend may have walked out on you, but when you worry about moments that have passed or have yet to occur, the Opponent has succeeded in keeping you away from the now, from a sense of safety. And the now is the one place in which the Opponent has no power.

QUICK SYSTEM REBOOT: EXERCISE #4

Before moving on, I'd like to do an exercise together. In fact, if you haven't done the exercises in the previous chapters, I encourage you to pause here, go back, and complete the prior exercises. Again, it's vital to put pen to paper; this action alone is a proactive one that places you in the present and hence in alignment with the Light of the Creator. We must practice action if we want to reveal Light.

When we're depressed, we often feel as if the weight of the universe is on our shoulders. We feel worried and anxious, or perhaps we shut down completely and feel very little at all. Take a moment and write down some of the concerns that are on your mind. If you're having trouble feeling much of anything, act *as if* you're worried. What would you be worried about? What are some people or situations that are dragging you down? Jot them down in the space provided:

_____

_____

_____

_____

_____

REBOOTING

_____

_____

_____

_____

_____

_____

_____

_____

_____

_____

Now take a moment to review your list. Which of the items on your list are events or situations that took place in the past? Are there items on your list that haven't happened at all or that you are anticipating will take place in the future? Draw a line through items that occurred in the past or have yet to take place. What items are left? Are these people or situations that you are dealing with directly at this exact moment? Or are you doing okay *in this moment*? Are your basic needs being met *here and now*? Do you have, *in this instant*, opportunities for growth and change? Because the truth of the matter is that this singular moment is all that matters, and the only thing preventing us from experiencing it fully is the Opponent. When we find ourselves living in the past or the future, consider it a red flag that the Opponent is at the helm again. A quick tweak in our thinking, such as what we just practiced in this written exercise, helps open our Vessel immediately and channel more Light our way.

PART FIVE

OVERCOMING
DEPRESSION

Okay, now it's time to get down to brass tacks. We've discussed the symptoms of depression, its source, and the obstacles that we face in conquering it. This information is significant, because all of it leads us to one question: How exactly do we overcome this insidious illness? In this section, we'll learn the kabbalistic tools that will enable us to pull depression up by its roots and expose it to the Light. And according to Kabbalah, anything that comes in contact with the Light and its transformative power—*anything*—becomes Light itself.

LOVING THY NEIGHBOR

We've all heard the old adage: "love thy neighbor as thyself."
According to Kabbalah, this singular principle offers more
insight into how we can achieve happiness than we could possibly imagine. In fact, all the teachings of Kabbalah can be
encapsulated in this one potent piece of divine advice. Its message is simple yet surprisingly profound, and at the heart of it
is the principle of sharing. Let me rephrase this—it's not the
principle of sharing; it's the *act* of sharing. Only when we emotionally and physically reach out to others and share can we
recover from depression.

The reason for this is simple. The nature of the Creator, according to Kabbalah, is an all-sharing, all-giving, all-loving force that
wants to fill our Vessel, our cup, continuously. But in order for
us to receive from this source, we need to be in affinity with it,
as we mentioned earlier. Therefore, the secret of the world is
that sharing is the ultimate cure-all. Yet if that is the case,
what's so wrong with the Creator just sharing and sharing with
us? The answer is that our nature is separate and different from
that of the Creator. We are receivers, remember? But we need
to be of one and the same nature in order for the Light force to
rest with us. So we must constantly transform our selfish nature
into a sharing one in order to receive.

**It is the ultimate paradox of life:
in order to receive, we must share.**

But what does it really mean to share and, more specifically, to share with your neighbor? Does it simply mean that when our neighbor wants to borrow the proverbial cup of sugar, we should give it to them? According to Kabbalah, the answer is no. While we certainly shouldn't begrudge our neighbor the cup of sugar, sharing—in its real sense—requires more of us. "More?" you might ask. Yes, more.

**According to Kabbalah, sharing occurs when we go
outside of our comfort zone to help another.**

When we act within our comfort zone or give someone something that we were going to throw out anyway, this might qualify as a good deed, but it's not sharing in the kabbalistic sense. The truth is that the more we must stretch ourselves to give, the more Light we receive. The more selfless our sharing, the greater our connection to the Light. And this reminds me of something my father has always said:

**When you get busy worrying about the welfare of
others, the Light gets busy worrying about you.**

But sharing requires that we make ourselves vulnerable to others; it requires that we feel. And the Opponent will do everything in his power to convince you that numbness (or hoarding your gifts) is preferable to feeling (or sharing). He will try to persuade you that comfort is what it's all about, even when it starts to feel a lot like numbness. In the moment that we share—the moment that we give away something we want or think we need—we begin to feel less numb, and we begin to transform from the inside out. Our defenses soften, and we begin to help others soften theirs. And this isn't just spiritual mumbo-jumbo. Medical studies show that the neurotransmitter patterns within the brains of depressed people were significantly altered when they volunteered to help others. In fact, helping others improved their depression more than any other treatment studied-including medications and therapy.

"Classically, what happens with depression," says psychotherapist Jamie Greene, a member of the Southern California Psychoanalytic Institute, "is that people with depression isolate. They stop having relationships. They collapse into themselves." Greene has been treating depression for 16 years. Six years ago he was introduced to Kabbalah and has been using it to treat patients ever since: "I found that with my depressed patients, Kabbalah helped them immensely. But the most imperative facet of the practice was sharing. Once they were involved in some kind of community project, they began to see some meaning and purpose in life, and they started to get out of bed early in the morning. Spiritually, they're connecting to the Light because they are sharing, so they actually start to come off medication. It's a process. It takes time, but it's impressive."

This type of transformation is happening to real people. Let's consider Shannon's story.

> "About a year ago, I was sinking into the worst depression of my life. I felt as if nothing about me was beautiful—not my mind, my soul, my body, or my heart. I would spend time mulling over how well everybody else's lives were running. I was aware of their troubles, but I always told myself that my life was harder. Maybe Rachel didn't make enough money or Marnie kept being dumped by her boyfriends, but at least Rachel had a boyfriend and Marnie had money. I didn't have either! No matter what anybody told me about their lives and no matter how much genuine compassion I might feel for them, ultimately I could always point out ways in which my life was worse.
>
> "One morning I walked past a community center with signs posted in the window for tutors.

Spontaneously I entered and volunteered to help eight and nine year olds with their homework two days a week. The very first time I did it, I felt different inside. Beforehand I was nervous: What if the kid didn't like me? What if I got a bad kid? What if I couldn't remember eighth grade math? As I've learned from studying Kabbalah, these are all egocentric fears! But the moment the tutoring started, I was transported so far away from my worries, it was like landing in heaven. For one hour, all of my energy went into helping somebody else with their life. And it wasn't a matter of pumping up my sense of self by feeling superior; rather, it was my heart that began to pump again! My depression began to lift for longer and longer stretches. Today I still struggle with depression, but far less intensely. And if I feel a particularly bad bout coming on, I know to pick up the phone, call someone, and say 'What can I do for you?' "

Shannon experienced firsthand what giving of one's self for the sake of another can do—it instantly multiplies the size of our Vessel and the desire we have for life, love, and Light. Remember that even small acts of selfless compassion lead to big Light-filled rewards at the end of the day.

PRACTICING APPRECIATION

Why do we find it so difficult to reach out and share? Because the Opponent convinces us that we have nothing of value to offer. Combating this false belief starts with a simple principle: appreciation.

Appreciation is integral to revealing Light in our lives. Without appreciation, all the wonderful people and situations in our lives would slip by unnoticed. We could have the whole world at our feet, but if we failed to appreciate these gifts, it would be as though we had nothing at all. In fact, according to Kabbalah, the act of appreciation is actually a Vessel in itself that holds Light. When we have appreciation for something, we can receive the Light that is inherent within it. Conversely, if we lack appreciation, we will never get fulfillment from what we do have.

Imagine an abundantly wealthy person who has no appreciation for money. Nothing he has, receives, or purchases brings him any satisfaction, fulfillment, or security. If this is the case, then the man might as well possess nothing at all. That's because the key to fulfillment lies not in what you have but in how much you *appreciate* what you have. The more you appreciate your gifts, the more Light you bring into your world. Depression is existing in a state of no appreciation.

The solution lies in becoming consciously aware of our gifts and blessings and maintaining a spirit of gratitude. This can be challenging when we are caught up in the temptations and pleasures of the 1% Realm. Why? Because when we are connected to this reality, we are usually looking only for our next temporary fix. But whatever fleeting pleasure we may attain in this way soon turns into pain. True appreciation consists not of the fleeting pleasure that attaches to a moment or an object, but of the real nature, meaning, and value of that moment or object. These are rarely aspects we can touch.

For instance, if a child makes you a special card, can you touch the time, love, and joy that went into creating it? The card itself is tangible, but it is merely a physical manifestation of the child's love for you. If we accept the card as only a card, then we will derive meaningful but temporary pleasure from the child's efforts. But if we go deeper, seeking to understand and appreciate the card as an expression of the child's essence, then we will have richer, more lasting joy, and so will he or she.

When we first start to build our Vessel by practicing appreciation, we may have to fake it a lot of the time. We might also have to take baby steps, as we discussed earlier. But the more we do so, the more our Vessel will grow, and the more Light we will experience. And believe me—it just keeps getting better and better until the darkness is banished completely, as you will soon see for yourself.

Try this exercise one morning. When you are dressing, consider all the care and effort that went into sewing your shirt, your pants, your underwear, and your socks. First someone grew the cotton; another gathered it, and yet another spun it. Someone else then wove it into fabric, which was then wound into a bolt and shipped to a factory, where someone else spent many hours cutting a pattern and sewing it on a machine or perhaps by hand. Then it was pressed and wrapped in protective plastic or perhaps folded into a box and shipped to a store. Here your piece of clothing was unpacked, steamed, and carefully displayed on the selling floor, waiting for a salesperson to present it to you. A lot of effort and energy went into your shirt!

So rather than simply throwing it on in the morning and tossing it in the laundry or on the floor at night, take a moment to appreciate all that went into the making of this single shirt. By doing this, you are actually connecting to the bigger picture behind what seems to be, at first blush, a simple item of clothing. Attaining this larger perspective builds your Vessel's capacity to hold Light. You are seeing beyond the confines of your personal existence by experiencing the interconnectivity of all of humankind. All of that by doing one small exercise!

I probably don't need to mention that appreciation is often difficult to tap into when we are feeling down and sorry for ourselves. But there are ways to overcome this initial resistance. Over the years, many students at The Kabbalah Centres have found it helpful to keep an "appreciation journal" in which they make daily lists of what they appreciate in themselves and in their lives. Or, some students choose to place sticky notes with the word *appreciate* around their homes to serve as gentle reminders. This activity encourages students to take a moment to run through all that they appreciate while staying focused on the now—not what they have appreciated in the past or what they expect to appreciate in the future, but what they appreciate *in that very moment*. It might be as basic as appreciating that you have food, water, and shelter, or that you had the energy to collect your mail that day; no gift or task is too small to list. However, it's important to do this exercise daily, even if you are repeating items, as it helps us train our minds to look for what we have in our lives rather than what we think we lack. And eventually this chore of listing what we are grateful for will become more easily accessed internally. It is well worth the time and effort. After all, have you ever met someone who was full of gratitude and depressed at the same time? Probably not. That's because appreciation and depression cannot coexist.

QUICK SYSTEM REBOOT: EXERCISE #5

Let's do a short exercise that is guaranteed to leave your system feeling restored. We're going to go on a scavenger hunt, but don't worry; I'm not going to require that you leave your comfy couch or bed (unless you want to). In fact, *you* are in charge of creating the list of items that are to be located. I want you to look around the room you are in. I want you to consider the pet that might be sleeping nearby or a child or partner who is close at hand. If you are alone, look at the pictures on the walls; thumb through the phone numbers and contacts in your cell phone; look at your appointment book if you keep one; or think about your current job, coworker, or boss. Now I want you to create a list of at least five people or things for which you are grateful. Note: Small things count just as much as big ones. That means that on this list, having a clean shirt to put on this morning counts just as much as being the parent of a healthy child. Write down the items that come to mind in the space provided:

_____

_____

_____

_____

REBOOTING

With your list written, it's now time to go on the hunt. You're probably thinking, "What? I know exactly where everything is already. I'm the one who made the list." And that, my friend, is exactly the point. You don't have to move a muscle to switch gears from emotional discomfort to gratitude and joy. That's because choosing gratitude over depression does not require a physical hunt at all; it simply requires a change in perspective. This adjustment in how you view the world around you has the ability to cause an immediate switch from darkness to light, and yet it requires only minimal effort on your part.

OUR *TIKKUN*

Kabbalah teaches us that we are all born with mental, emotional, spiritual, and even physical baggage that we have dragged with us from previous lives. This baggage is the cumulative effect of all the times we failed to resist our reactive behavior. And because our baggage comes in all shapes and sizes, our personal *Tikkun* can manifest in all kinds of forms. For some it is a fear of public speaking; for others it is an uncanny knack for always picking the man who can't remain faithful: or always being the girl with the awesome potential who never made it that far. Whenever you recognize a repetitive pattern of behavior in yourself, you know you are facing your *Tikkun*. This is a reactive component of your personality that is no longer benefiting you—one that you will soon learn to transform into acts of sharing. As we learn to recognize our *Tikkun* and correct our negative patterns, we create opportunities for Light. And in the face of Light, our darkness begins to dissolve.

Our *Tikkun* plays a quintessential role in increasing our Vessel—*if* we recognize and correct it. Remember, our primary purpose in this life is to reconnect to the Light, and we do so by transforming, stretching, and growing. When we stretch and grow spiritually, our Vessel stretches and grows as well. And you know by now what a large Vessel can do for you; a large

REBOOTING

Vessel equates to bountiful Light. We make corrections and increase our Vessel by resisting the impulse to react hastily to challenging events in our path. When we identify our *Tikkun* and learn to control our reactions, we create permanent, lasting change.

OUR *TIKKUN* AND REINCARNATION

Let's take the principle of *Tikkun* one step further, for it is part of a much bigger picture of reincarnation and the traveling of the soul. Kabbalah tells us that we are all reincarnated souls. Many mysterious things begin to make a lot more sense when viewed through this lens! Most of us have had the experience of having visited a new place only to feel strongly that we've been there before. We even have a name for this: déjà vu. Or perhaps we've met someone new, and rather than feel as if we've known that person for only five minutes, we feel as though we've known them forever. Most of us have been taught to believe that we have one life and one life only. "Life is short," we might say, or "you only live once." But what if life is not short? What if this life is part of a long continuum of lives? Wouldn't that help explain those evocative sensations of déjà vu and familiar strangers?

Reincarnation would certainly help shed light on many of our seemingly irrational fears. Suppose we are afraid of heights—many people are—when nothing terrible has actually happened to us up high. Or we are afraid of boats, when nothing frightening has ever happened to us on a boat or even in water. Where, then, do these fears come from? According to Kabbalah, they reflect a traumatic experience that we suffered in a past life—

one in which we may have fallen from a great height or were injured in a boating accident and perhaps didn't make it to safety. These fears, carried over from previous lives, then become the fabric of our Tikkun—carryovers from past lives that we need to sort through in this one.

Let's talk money, for example. We all know people who have difficulty drawing financial abundance into their lives. Why might this be the case? Someone who has difficulty earning money in this life may well have been miserly in a previous one. This individual's desire to help others might have been minimal, and as a result, his or her Vessel has contracted. His or her *Tikkun* might be to learn to be generous and to help others. As soon as the individual overcomes his or her selfish nature and commits acts of true sharing, abundance will start flowing.

We all know the story of the stingy Ebenezer Scrooge in *A Christmas Carol.* What a perfect example of confronting one's Tikkun! After Mr. Scrooge recognized his repetitive behavior, he quickly made the necessary correction, and by doing so he experienced abundance, happiness, and a capacity to actually enjoy what he had in his life.

Our *Tikkun* is not bad. It is, in fact, necessary to our spiritual progress. Recognizing our *Tikkun* helps us see the kinds of choices we've made in this life and perhaps in past lives, serving as a crucial step in revealing Light. By seeing our *Tikkun* with clear eyes, we can hone in on those decisions that have brought us joy, as well as those that have not.

By understanding our personal Tikkun, we can:

- Identify our weaknesses so that we can overcome them;

- Recognize the baggage we're carrying from previous lives so we can unburden ourselves from it;

- Avoid roadblocks and detours that slow our progress toward the Light so that we can gain more direct access to the Light;

- Overcome our deepest fears so that we can understand where they came from, recognize that they are not a part of the here and now, and turn them into Light; and

- Take steps to realize our fullest potential in the most profound sense.

If we overcome those aspects of ourselves that we came into this world to overcome, we will be completely unshackled and will be able to soar to our greatest potential. Not bad for something we've been avoiding all these years!

Remember, there are no bad signs or bad moments or bad things that happen to us in this life—only different kinds of opportunities. If we can understand challenging events not as bad things but as opportunities for change, it will be easier for us to make our corrections, reveal Light, and conquer depression. This is an important point for us to understand. So many of us have struggled to find meaning in our lives—to find the "answer" that always seems to elude us—and the disappointments can be devastating. Making corrections helps end this struggle by leading us toward the Light. If you need assistance in understanding what *Tikkun* means and how it can help you grow, do not hesitate to call student support at 1-800-KABBALAH.

Before moving on, there's another aspect of depression and the traveling of souls that deserves our attention. Kabbalah teaches that when a person commits suicide, his or her soul is unable to ascend to the next level. The soul gets stuck, so to speak, in an intermediate dimension, where it begins searching for a resting place. Thoughts of suicide are a means of shutting down our Vessel; they are yet another way of closing ourselves off from the opportunities that life presents to us in order to reveal Light. When a person gives in to suicidal thoughts inspired by the Opponent, that person risks creating an opening through which a misplaced soul—what I call a "walk-in"— might enter. How is this possible? Remember the Law of Attraction? Like attracts like. Our suicidal thoughts attract souls who once experienced and acted on those thoughts. These souls may walk into our lives, and rest within us, thereby causing our symptoms of depression to intensify.

It is important to know that a person does not have to be suffering from major depression in order for this to occur. Even those with mild depression might allow their minds to entertain thoughts of suicide in order to gain the temporary energy that such an escape can provide. This creates a perfect opportunity for a walk-in, who will cause symptoms of mild depression to worsen disproportionately. That's because now, in addition to the individual's own depressed thinking, he or she has accumulated the negativity of the walk-in soul.

When a walk-in enters our life, we are not at its mercy. There are some steps we can take to remove this entity from our being:

- **Mikveh.** This is a ritual immersion in water. According to Kabbalah, water is a physical form of Light and carries great healing properties. By immersing ourselves in a pool of fresh water, we engulf ourselves in Light, thereby removing any traces of darkness.

- **Meditation.** Utilizing a powerful meditation called *Banishing Evil Thoughts and Remnants of Evil* may also prove beneficial. Simply scanning the ancient Aramaic letters associated with this meditation can bring relief from the presence of a walk-in soul. For more information, refer to my book *The 72 Names of God* or turn to Part Six of this book, where we discuss meditating on the 72 Names of God in more detail.

- **Student support.** If you feel you need more assistance, please call 1-800-KABBALAH.

QUICK SYSTEM REBOOT: EXERCISE #6

We all have situations, people, and patterns that appear in our lives again and again. Take a moment to think about your life. Do you see any patterns? Are there actions that you take repeatedly or people you allow into your life that cause you heartache? Recognizing tendencies in ourselves is the first step toward learning to correct them. And one of the keys to identifying such tendencies lies in being completely honest about the painful and repetitive situations that have occurred in our lives. There is no need to feel shame in this regard, for shame serves only to keep our *Tikkun* concealed. Now is the time to be open and honest with yourself. In the space provided, write down any patterns that you see.

_____

_____

_____

_____

_____

_____

_____

_____

TO REACT OR NOT TO REACT

Correcting our *Tikkun* starts with learning to resist our reactive tendencies. This is how we begin to reach our full potential as human beings and where the exciting stuff really starts to happen! One of the most useful tools Kabbalah has to offer is a method by which we can first identify our reactive behavior and then transform it into proactive behavior.

But what exactly is reactive behavior?

According to Kabbalah, we are being reactive any time we feel as if things are happening to us, no matter whether we respond to that sentiment with active or passive behavior. For example, thoughts that blame our unhappiness on external conditions are reactive. When we are reactive, we unconsciously shrink our Vessel, and with it our desire for life and Light.

And we withdraw further . . .

Each time we close that bedroom door—not because we need rest and relaxation, but because the Opponent is drawing us in—we are depriving someone somewhere of our generosity, our talents, and our own inherent ability to help them move through their pain toward the Light. This is reactive behavior.

PROACTIVELY HAPPENING
TO OURSELVES

Now that we're learning how to better recognize reactive behavior in ourselves, it's time we learned how to transform reactive behavior into something infinitely beneficial: proactive behavior. This is a term my father coined to describe any thoughts, words, or deeds we engage in that challenge our base nature.

When we act proactively, we recognize that nothing is ever happening *to* us; we are in charge of ourselves. And if I am happening to me—good or bad—then I am connecting with the 99% Realm. And here is a critically important point to remember:

Every time we share, we behave proactively, and every time we restrict our reactive impulses, we are behaving proactively. This is because when we behave proactively, we are acting as the Light of the Creator acts.

Reactive behavior, on the other hand, serves only to invite darkness and depression. In order to understand this better, let's revisit the idea of cause and effect. If we succumb to reactive behavior when dealing with events and people, we become the effect of our impulses rather than the *cause* of our own lives. When we behave in this manner, we lose our affinity with the

Creator, the Cause of all things wonderful. By shifting our attention to proactive behavior, we become the Cause. We become creators. And by becoming the Cause, we are in affinity with the Light.

WHAT DO I REALLY WANT?

Are you ready to become the creator of your life and eliminate depression forever? If your answer is yes, then it's time to learn and practice the simple yet profound act of pausing before reacting. Why is it so hard to pause for one moment before reacting? You might have guessed it: because the Opponent makes it hard. Very hard. In the face of any situation, whether it offers us pleasure or pain, the Opponent urges us to react without thinking. He wants us to give in to our reactive nature. Why? Because when we do, we disconnect from the 99% Realm and from all the Light it offers. And that's exactly where the Opponent wants us to be: alone in the dark.

By pausing to consider our reactions and by choosing to be a conscious and present participant in our lives, we can begin to experience amazing relief from our depression. This means that we will cease to run on autopilot and will stop responding to provocations out of habit. Relying on old patterns of operation will not lead us out of the darkness, but creating a gap between a stimulus and your response will—for it is during this gap that you have the opportunity to ask a pivotal question:

WHAT DO I REALLY WANT?

Asking this simple question prompts us to uncover our heart's true desires. For example, if we are considering a one-night stand, do we want the sex, or do we want a genuine emotional connection with someone who loves us and whom we love? If it's money we're after, is it the cash or a sense of security that we truly desire? Today, many people are undergoing plastic surgery. Are such people seeking to transform their bodies or their self-esteem? Asking this simple question: What do I really want?—leads us to the realization that our heart's true desires are never temporary and fleeting—like winning an argument or putting someone in his or her place. What we really want are lasting connections with those around us. By pausing to consider our responses carefully, we are far less likely to choose reactions that will leave us feeling empty again in a matter of seconds. By asking this question, you give the Light an opportunity to pour into your Vessel and guide your response. It is only by resisting your impulse to throw an angry punch that you create possibilities for joy and true satisfaction.

By the way, taking a moment to consider a response doesn't necessarily mean that we can't respond. After pausing, we may still decide to take an action—even a tough one—on our own behalf. For instance, the woman who cut in front of us in line probably doesn't warrant our attention, but the guy at work who stole our idea might. And there would be nothing wrong with trying to remedy the situation. According to Kabbalah, everything happens for a reason. In this instance, rather than shutting down and feeling as if life is happening to us, speaking to our coworker might provide him with an opportunity to discover his own gifts. Or it may turn out that our colleague is having personal problems that are causing him to act out in a reckless and disrespectful manner. By being present in the situation, we might discover ways we can share—and by sharing, we reveal even more Light. Plus, it might lead to an amazing friendship. The possibilities contained in proactive behavior are limitless.

I recently spoke with a woman who said that many of her most meaningful relationships began with her disliking the person. Her critical eye had been keeping her from developing worthwhile connections with those around her. Clearly, this was an indicator of her Tikkun. But the woman was able to transform the energy of her initial reaction into proactive behavior. And by behaving proactively, she was able to lift the curtain and reveal the Light. Kabbalah shows us how to transform the energy we bring to our responses. Tough situations will always arise; that is something over which we have no control. But what we *can* control is how we greet them.

PUTTING IT ALL TOGETHER

You've learned a great deal of useful information thus far. Let's now take a moment to put it all together. Kabbalah offers a step-by-step Transformation Formula to help us turn our reactive behavior into proactive behavior. It looks like this:

1. An obstacle occurs.

2. Identify the real enemy. Realize that our reaction (the Opponent)—not the obstacle—is the real enemy, and that the Opponent is, in fact, our ego.

3. Shut down your reactive system. This makes room to allow the Light in.

4. Express your proactive nature. See yourself as the cause, as the creator, as a being who shares.

The moment of transformation takes place during steps three and four. This is the point at which we are able to plug into the 99% Realm, when we can touch the Light.

Let's see how the Transformation Formula might apply to a real-life situation. Suppose your friend invites you to a party. She tells you that there will be lots of single people there. You have been alone for a long time and would truly like to have someone to date again. You think that having someone special in your life might help lift your spirits. The night before the party you don't sleep well, although you are exhausted. At work the next day, you think about the party and how much you want to go, but then you imagine having to talk to complete strangers and being unable to come up with anything interesting to say. When you get home, you think you'll eat dinner and then have a shower and get dressed, but after you eat you decide to watch your favorite TV show. When that's over, you look at your clothes and realize that your only appropriate shirt is dirty. Nothing else fits properly. And your lower back is starting to hurt again, so it probably makes more sense for you to rest and take care of yourself than to go out on the town. Although it would certainly be nice to meet someone special, you'd rather wait for a night when you have something worthwhile to say and feel a little better about yourself. Plus, there's something so comforting and reassuring about the thought of slipping between those warm sheets with a big bowl of buttered popcorn and the remote control!

At first glance, this may not seem like reactive behavior, because it's so passive. Where is the abusive behavior? Where is the violent anger? But let's apply the formula we just learned to this situation and see how it might turn out differently if we connect with the Light and resist the Opponent.

1. *An obstacle occurs.* You are invited to a party. The opportunity it poses challenges you to move beyond the comfort zone you've established for your life. It threatens the safe haven you've created for your emotions and from the hopes and fears—or desires—you've suppressed.

2. *Identify the real enemy.* Recognize that your reaction is the real enemy. Your lack of desire is what you truly need to battle, not the prospect of going to a party.

3. *Shut down your reactive system* to allow the Light in. There is a split-second pause before we make any decision—even the most spontaneous one—in which we choose how to respond. The more control we exercise over our reactive behavior, the greater access we have to that moment of choice. When we find ourselves lacking in intellect, or attractiveness, or ability, we are being reactive. Judging anyone—including ourselves—is reactive behavior. So the moment you sabotage your desire to go to the party over concerns about how you'll look, you are engaging in reactive behavior. Not react-

ing quickly to those concerns, or taking a moment to realize that you really would like to go, is a way of taking responsibility for your life. In this case, it is a way to allow your deeper desire to be honored.

4. *Express your proactive nature.* See yourself as the cause, as the creator, as a being who shares. Remember that one important way to fight depression and to draw in the Light is by sharing. And the only way you can share is by interacting with others, right? Fighting depression requires action. When we are depressed, our minds, bodies, and souls stagnate. We reinvigorate our desire by taking a considered action. Going to the party awakens the desire for companionship, sharing, kindness, and perhaps even physical intimacy. All good stuff. Once our desire is flowing again, our depression begins to lift.

I've seen the four steps of the Transformation Formula work time and time again.

Harry had been struggling with depression for nearly 20 years when he came to one of our Kabbalah Centres. Harry "self-medicated" his depression by abusing recreational drugs and alcohol. He was also terrified of being alone. Depression does not always manifest in solitary behavior; plenty of people who suffer from it create ongoing chaos in their lives because they are so afraid of being alone. Remember that facing your depression—identifying it and taking responsibility for it—is the first step toward healing. Harry took to the Transformation Formula like dew to morning grass. Here is what he had to say:

> *"I had tried every drug prescribed and stolen, not to mention all the alcohol and cigarettes. I had some good nights—some great nights, in fact— but over time the mornings-after became increasingly painful. For a while, I killed that pain with more drugs. Then I got off the heroin, gave up the alcohol, and began moving from antidepressant to antidepressant, trying to find the one that would calm me and invigorate me at the same time. All the while, a big hole dug its way deeper inside of me. Once I stopped partying, a lot of 'friends' didn't want to hang out with me, so I began spending more and more time alone. This was not good for me! I'm a thinker, and all I did was think about how awful my life was; not only that, I would think about how awful everybody's life was. I couldn't sleep anymore, and it wasn't long before I was back on the heroin, back at the bars, back to hanging out with nonstop company. At least this way, I could limit how much pain I had to feel."*

"By studying the Transformation Formula, I began to recognize some of my behavior. It turns out that most drug addicts are just chasing after the Light. We call it a high, but in a lot of ways it's the same feeling. I was just going after this feeling in a way that couldn't last. My obstacle was the drugs, but they were just the effect. My real enemy was my fear of being alone with my depression, with that big black hole that had taken over what used to be my heart. My reaction to this was, naturally, to do some more drugs. I had a desire to hide from my own pain, and drugs were an effect of this desire. I knew that every time I went for the drugs, I was being reactive.

"Slowly I started making changes. Instead of going out to the bars, I invited a good pal over to dinner, and we spoke at length about how it felt to be depressed. It turned out that she struggled with depression too, though she was never at the parties I went to because she was too busy lying under her comforter watching TV. She told me later how important it had been for her to get out of the house to have dinner with me, to resist some of her own reactive behavior. So by recognizing my obstacle and choosing to resist my *reactive behavior, I not only helped myself but helped someone else. Later I learned that this was a form of sharing, and one of the key tools to overcoming depression.*

"From that night forward, even though nothing had changed dramatically, I began working the Transformation Formula every chance I could. It's been four years now. I am 100% clean, no antidepressants, and while I still enjoy the company of others, I am able to sit with myself and with any areas of discomfort or pain that might need addressing. While it's always hard to face painful parts of myself, I can do so now knowing it's the first step toward transforming them into desire and Light."

Kabbalah teaches that there are two ways to remove the curtains that obscure the Light: suffering and spiritual transformation. When we suffer, the actual hurting involved—the pain, the grief, the heartache—produces a kind of catharsis. It purges the ego, after which our soul—or true self—shines more brightly. This is why we can experience a sudden sense of unity and love with others after a tragedy, or why we may feel better after a good cry. The experience of profound suffering subdues our ego and touches our soul.

However, the Light experienced through suffering is usually only temporary in nature. As the memory of the pain fades, our soul retreats, and our ego once again feels confident enough to tempt us into reacting to its impulses. Watch for the moments in which the ego is playing cat and mouse. Pause and monitor your response. The Transformation Formula is the key to awakening your desires.

WILLINGNESS

You can read this book ten times, underline meaningful passages, and encourage friends to experiment with the Transformation Formula, but without a genuine and profound willingness to change, nothing will be accomplished. Willingness is not a surface emotion. It's not the same as wanting something, for instance. Wants can be fleeting, encompassing everything from new tennis shoes to a pink bathroom to a better lover. You can want something until you are blue in the face, but without a willingness to take the necessary steps to achieve it, everything will remain the same.

If you are reading this book, there is little doubt that you want to let go of your depression. This is good, by the way, because it means that you are experiencing desire—and that your lack of desire is beginning to lift. Excellent. However, consider whether you are really willing to let your depression go. It is human nature to become set in our ways. Even our most detrimental tendencies can seem comforting simply because they are familiar. What would it feel like to *not* be depressed? What might happen if desires crept up? Might they encourage us to do things we're not prepared to do? Might they push us harder than we are prepared to go? Wouldn't not being depressed bring with it its own complications—ones that might be even worse than those we are experiencing now? What will facing our *Tikkun* be like? Take a moment to really consider these questions. We might not like being depressed, but at least we know how to do it. How can we do something we've never experienced? We are often afraid of change. Change brings with it a completely new set of emotions, and we've barely made peace with the old set. So a strong sense of willingness is essential if we are to change in any meaningful or lasting way. But don't worry; I'll show you how to strengthen your will.

There is a traditional kabbalistic teaching that goes like this:

A student, feeling he had committed unfathomable wrongs, went to his teacher and confessed. His teacher, who was a great kabbalist, told the student that the things he had done were so horrendous that the only possible means of atonement would be an agonizing death: He was to pour hot mercury down his throat. At first, the student was devastated and filled with fear. There were many things in his life that he did not want to leave, and he certainly did not welcome a painful, drawn-out death. But after much soul searching, the student agreed. However, he asked his teacher to administer the poison for him, as he was unable to do so himself.

The kabbalist instructed the student to lie on his back, close his eyes, and open his mouth. The student did as he was asked, and his teacher poured a cool liquid down his throat. Expecting to be in the throes of death, the student was startled to find himself very much alive! The liquid had been nothing more than water. The kabbalist explained that because the student had been willing to die in order to atone for his sins—because he had faced the greatest fear of all, the fear of dying—all the negative traits that had caused him to commit the horrendous acts in the first place had been transformed into Light!

What is the message of this story? The need for willingness. The student didn't merely want to atone for his misdeeds; he was *willing* to do so. He had a determination and clarity that came from deep within his soul. In order for us to change, we need to find this same willingness—this same sense of determination and clarity—within ourselves.

PART SIX

RESOURCES
THAT HEAL

The technology of Kabbalah contains a wealth of proven resources and practices that will help you on your journey out of depression. By keeping these resources at the tips of your fingers, you will help keep darkness at bay. Let's discuss a few of these time-honored tools.

THE ZOHAR

THE KABBALISTIC CALENDAR

THE 72 NAMES OF GOD

WATER

BURNING

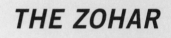

THE ZOHAR

THE ZOHAR

The Zohar, the quintessential text of Kabbalah was written over 2,000 years ago in Aramaic and contains the mystical commentary of the Torah. The word *Zohar* means "radiance" or "splendor' in Aramaic, which is why *The Zohar* is also known as *The Book of Splendor*. *The Zohar* is like a candle in this world of darkness. It transcends religion, race, gender, politics, and geography. All darkness, no matter how penetrating it may be, gives way to the power of Light, even if its source is a single candle.

What can this ancient text do for you? The simple act of scanning *The Zohar*—running our eyes over its sequences of letters—can ignite a tremendous healing energy within us even if it is done for only five or ten minutes a day. All of the great kabbalists engaged in this practice, crediting it with powerful breakthroughs both in themselves and in their students. As we scan *The Zohar*, we let our minds contemplate what it means to awaken desire, remove our blocks, and heal our fears. Rest assured that your ego will try to convince you that scanning passages written in a language you cannot read couldn't possibly have a positive effect on your well-being. Take care to ignore this voice. The ego distracts us time and again with its argument that logic is the only form of understanding. Such nonsense! Powers of understanding exist within the realm of logic—this is true. But countless others exist in realms we can't see, hear, touch, smell, or taste. Try scanning *The Zohar* once each morning and again before bed. If you feel improvements, keep scanning every day.

Let me share with you a story about a student of mine. About ten years ago, Elliott came to me complaining that she was having trouble sleeping. She woke up each night at around 2:00 AM feeling especially depressed and empty, and she couldn't fall asleep again for hours. By the time we met, Elliott was so run down that she was having trouble functioning at work. We discussed how it was the Opponent (her own ego) who was waking her each night and tormenting her with negative thoughts. She then decided that the next time it happened, she would meditate on *The Zohar*. Sure enough, the following morning she woke up at 2:00 AM—but this time she scanned *The Zohar*, focusing on awakening her desires, and soon she began to feel sleepy.

Elliott did the same thing the next night and for several more nights after that. Finally, after two weeks of reading *The Zohar* when she woke up in the night, her ego realized that by interrupting her sleep, it was actually feeding a good habit—one that released tremendous Light and diminished its power. So the Opponent stopped. Elliott has been sleeping well ever since. And her practice of scanning with the intention of reinvigorating her desire not only allowed her to sleep but profoundly changed her waking hours as well. Elliott began to seek out companionship and became more excited about her job. After several more months of daily scanning, she was promoted. Elliott has continued the practice of scanning *The Zohar* daily and has been enjoying her life more each day as a result.

THE KABBALISTIC
CALENDAR

THE KABBALISTIC CALENDAR

The Zohar contains a valuable component which we can also use as a resource to overcome depression: the kabbalistic calendar.

According to *The Zohar*, the calendar is not a way to mark the passing of time. Rather, it is a tool to help us identify the different energies and opportunities that exist in the universe.

Let's use an example from the physical world: gardening. When we are preparing a flower garden, we need to know the specific seasons during which we should plant the seeds for each type of flower. For instance, planting a rose bush in the dead of winter might be a bad idea, but other, hardier flowers may thrive in cooler weather. It's both beneficial and wise to be aware of these types of opportunities.

According to Kabbalah, "As above, so below." In other words, nothing can happen in the physical world that is not first dictated from above, or the 99% Realm. The kabbalistic calendar describes the various spiritual windows of time during which we can take advantage of opportunities that exist here in the physical realm—opportunities that affect everything from physical health to spiritual development. There are certain times when we can plant seeds to meet soul mates, for instance. Conversely, there are times when it is advisable *not* to plant seeds for marriage or for the purchase of a family home. Additionally, there are times during the year in which healing is most likely to occur. But there also exists a period of time during which we need to be careful not to plant seeds that could result in destruction or disease.

One of the key pitfalls to be wary of during the month of Cancer, which falls between July and August, is depression. Did you ever notice that there are particular times of the year when you are more inclined to be depressed? Well, according to the kabbalistic calendar, it is much more difficult to connect to the Light in the month of Cancer, because the Light is cosmically in a state of concealment at this time. This creates a greater potential for depression and requires a more concerted effort on our part to connect to the Light during this period.

The potential for activating cancer cells in the body also increases during this time. Kabbalists explain that in the course of this month, we can unwittingly plant a seed for disease that might not show up for many years, making it difficult for us to connect the cause with the effect. As you might remember, this is the Opponent at work. The Opponent loves to use time to confuse us and to lead us to believe that life is chaotic and random. But you know now that this is simply not the case!

REBOOTING

The Zohar and the kabbalistic calendar provide us with some incredibly useful information to help us counter the Opponent's tricks. *The Zohar* is literally arming us with the knowledge that during the month of Cancer, we are susceptible to depression as well as at risk of inadvertently planting the seed of cancer. It's as if *The Zohar* intentionally fed us the Opponent's battle plan! Armed with this knowledge, we can do our utmost to be positive and to share during that time in order to divert depression and disease!

It's not surprising that medical science is now discovering what kabbalists said more then 2,000 years ago—that there is a close connection between depression and other illnesses. In fact, there is a new branch of science called psychoneuroimmunology that is dedicated to exploring the connection between the mind and the immune system. By actively incorporating the wisdom of the kabbalistic calendar into our daily existence, we can fortify our immune systems and eliminate disease and depression from our lives completely.

THE 72 NAMES OF GOD

THE 72 NAMES OF GOD

The same kind of profound healing energy is available to us through the 72 Names of God. These are not names in the ordinary sense. Rather, the 72 Names of God are a life force—a complete technology of healing, protection, and positive change—that was originally revealed in *The Zohar*. The Names are, in fact, more powerful than any means of healing yet discovered in the 21st century. This is because they function at the DNA level of the soul, or what physicists refer to as the quantum level of reality. The Names contain the power to remove any interference that may block us from our desires. When the interference is gone, we can connect once more with what we truly desire.

As you might have guessed, there are 72 Names in total. If you are interested in learning about all of them, you are welcome to review my book *The 72 Names of God* or visit www.72.com. There are specific Names that combat the lure of the Opponent in relation to depression. We've provided a list of some of the specific Names and their corresponding meditations in the upcoming pages.

The 72 Names of God are formed from 22 Aramaic letters that contain enormous amounts of spiritual energy. These are not names in the traditional sense and are often not pronounceable in any recognizable manner. Moreover, the specific configurations of the three-letter sequences of the 72 Names are devoid of any literal meaning. Yet they unleash a sacred and profoundly influential force when we visualize them and meditate on using that force in our lives.

In fact, the Aramaic word for *letter* actually means "pulse" or "vibration." As you view these letters, you are interacting with their pulses, or energies. Different combinations create different energies just as different combinations of musical notes create different tunes. Each Name contains infinite amounts of positive, healing energy that we can access any time we need.

Don't worry if you are unable to read Aramaic, because it is the energetic vibrations to which you want to connect, not the intellectual information of the meanings. These 72 Names are universal symbols whose power and spiritual energy transcend distinctions based on religion, race, class, gender, or geography—indeed, all external classifications. The healing vibrations of the 72 Names are intended for the soul, and the soul recognizes no such distinctions. Simply scanning the letters from right to left transmits their power.

REBOOTING

There are three prerequisites to activating the power of the 72 Names of God:

1. Conviction in their power;

2. An understanding of the particular influence radiating from each Name; and

3. A follow-through physical action to activate their power.

The first prerequisite is entirely up to you. Your ego will again resort to logic to try to make you doubt the power of these letters! And your depression might tell you that it's easier to do nothing than to struggle against your doubt. At this juncture, it is important to remember that the more reactive we remain, the more powerful our ego becomes. Certainty is proactive. It is a form of willingness and a desire. Engaging in and winning this battle is how you will find the Light.

The second prerequisite is provided for you. The spiritual influence and power of the five Names that are especially helpful in overcoming depression are now accessible to you after thousands of years of secrecy. Appreciating this fact will make your connection to the Light even stronger.

The third requirement, a follow-through action, is sometimes the hardest one to accomplish. If, for example, you are afraid of meeting new people, then you need to start a conversation with the lady behind you in the line for coffee. If you are afraid of heights, venture to the top of a tall building. Bring a friend, but take the action. Confront your fears, and then take the action they have previously prevented you from taking!

As you might have noticed, the foundation for the technology of the 72 Names is proactive behavior. Without this, even the most powerful technologies cannot work for us. But when we resist reactive behavior and embrace proactive words, thoughts, and actions, we ignite the power and healing energy of these Names.

MEDITATING ON THE 72 NAMES

Let's take a look at how you might meditate on one of the Names. As we have already discussed, meditation can have a profoundly healing effect on depression by helping us stay in the present moment. But it goes beyond that. We can meditate on specific Names that provide direct relief from depression by igniting desire and revealing Light.

Find a quiet setting—one where you are least likely to be disturbed by curious roommates, concerned partners, faithful pets, or bored friends. Then take a few moments to make sure the area is clean and neat. You want to be respectful of both yourself and the spiritual lineage of these letters. Now take a seat in a comfortable chair. It is best not to sit on the floor, because we are using these Names to elevate us, and sitting on the floor grounds us instead. Kabbalistic meditation should always be practiced while sitting with correct posture in a chair.

Now allow your eyes to gently rest on the letters with full attention, but without undue focus or concentration. Try not to let your attention wander or wane. Whenever it does, gently bring it back to the letters. Sometimes it is helpful to focus on your breathing—on inhaling and exhaling over and over. You can even imagine that you are inhaling the power of the letters and that this power is filling every molecule of your body. Then, when you exhale, imagine you are exhaling the power out for others to access. Then breathe in the power once more—try visualizing it in the form of white light—and let it fill you. Keep doing this until your breathing and visualizations feel natural and easy. Then close your eyes and see the letters in your mind's eye. Try to imagine them as vividly as possible, just as if you were looking at them on the page. See the black letters outlined against a white background. Then open your eyes.

Once more, focus on the letters. Use your breathing practice to inhale and exhale the Light. Continue this for a comfortable interval. Close your eyes once again and visualize the letters, but this time imagine them as white against a black background. Let them fill your mind as completely as possible. If other thoughts or images arise, don't get upset; just return to your breathing until they drift away. Be aware now that the letters are no longer on the paper; they are within you! Now, open your eyes. Resist the urge to study the letters some more. For the time being, the printed letters are irrelevant. The letters are within you now. Actually, they've always been within you; they've simply been reawakened.

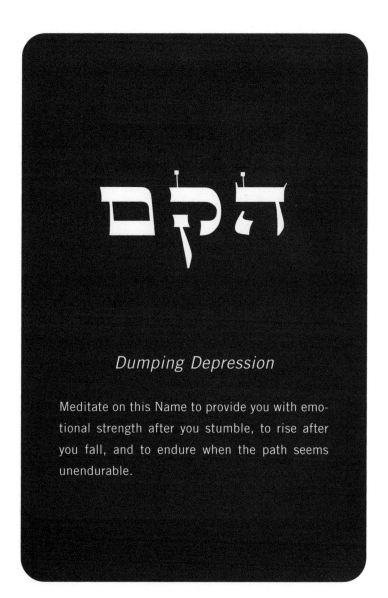

הקם

Dumping Depression

Meditate on this Name to provide you with emotional strength after you stumble, to rise after you fall, and to endure when the path seems unendurable.

Self-Esteem

Meditate on this Name to establish your own direct connection to the Light within you and to achieve the power to solve your own problems.

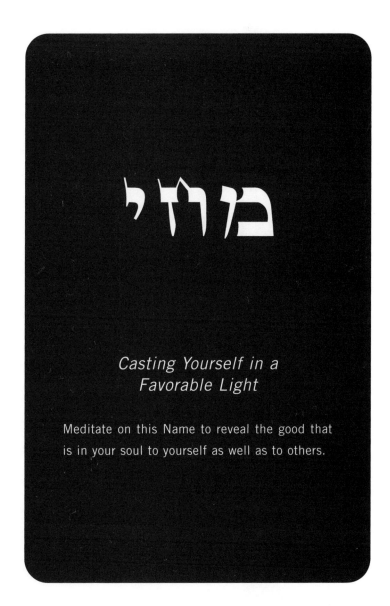

מוזי

*Casting Yourself in a
Favorable Light*

Meditate on this Name to reveal the good that
is in your soul to yourself as well as to others.

Recognizing Design Beneath Disorder

Meditate on this Name to achieve profound understanding of cause and effect, and to instill acceptance of hardships and chaotic circumstances as opportunities for spiritual elevation. Meditate on this name to expand your desire and grow to your greatest potential.

Accountability

Meditate on this Name to rid yourself of the belief that you can't control what happens to you and to replace that belief with the knowledge that you are the creator of your own circumstances. Whatever you have created—good or bad—you can change.

Recapturing the Sparks

Meditate on this Name to regain the lost sparks
of spiritual Light that belong in your soul.

REBOOTING

עמם

Passion

Meditate on this Name to stoke the fires of passion in your heart and in your soul and to reinvigorate your desires.

WATER

WATER

Water has tremendous healing powers. *Mikveh*, or the bath of immersion, is a traditional purification ritual that has been used for thousands of years in connection with cleansing, removing negativity, healing, and preparing our internal Vessel to receive Light. It is a powerful tool in overcoming depression. Rav Akiva's life was inextricably altered by the power of water. In addition, drinking clean, filtered water can also improve depressive states. Abram Ber, M.D., shares his experience:

> *"A patient came to see me several years ago suffering from depression. None of the drugs given to her by her psychiatrist had any long-lasting benefits. After I had treated her for some months with no amelioration, I referred her to a therapist, who on the first visit asked her how much water she drank in one day. She replied that on an average day, she drank two glasses of water. He advised her to rehydrate her body by drinking ten glasses of water per day, and lo and behold, her depression was vastly improved within a week. Needless to say, it was a lesson I never needed repeating. Now I ask every patient how many glasses of water he or she drinks per day."*

We mustn't overlook the healing properties of water. Most experts recommend a minimum of six to eight 8-ounce glasses of water per day. The best approach is to drink one glass one half-hour before each meal, followed by a similar amount two and one-half hours after each meal. This is the very minimum your body needs! According to Dr. Fereydoon Batmanghelidj, author of *Water For Health, for Healing, for Life*, who spent 20 years researching the effects of dehydration, water is the cheapest form of medicine. Dr. Batmanghelidj writes, "Seventy-five percent of our bodies are composed of water. The brain is 85% water. It is water that energizes and activates the solid matter. If you don't take enough water, some functions of the body will suffer. Dehydration produces system disturbances. When I use the words *water cure*, I am referring to curing dehydration with water."

If we're not careful, a dehydrated mind can lead to a depressed mind. By introducing sufficient amounts of water, our minds can become fluid again, giving us greater ability to recognize and awaken our desires.

BURNING

BURNING

Burning is yet another powerful healing tool available to us. One of the greatest kabbalists of all times, Isaac Luria, developing this simple yet potent technique for transforming negativities. He suggested lighting a candle and sitting before it with a pencil and a small piece of paper. Write down a key word regarding your depression, such as loneliness, incompetence, or failed love, or jot down a short sentence describing exactly how you feel. I suggest that you always include "lack of desire" on the list. Briefly meditate on your depression. You are trying to carefully yet thoroughly dredge up all the feelings associated with it. Now write these down as well. Next, acknowledge to yourself that your own reactive nature, be it from this life or a past life, is responsible for the manifestation of this depression in your life. Now, take the paper and burn it! You will be surprised how this symbolic act can eliminate your emotional blocks and free your trapped energy.

ON HOPE

My greatest hope with this book is that it can convey my belief—and that of Kabbalah—that life is not hopeless, and that we have more power to bring excitement and beauty into our lives than we ever dreamed possible. That power comes from the Light of the Creator. It doesn't get much better than that! The Opponent, as always, will try his best to make you feel like nothing more than a pawn in the game of life. He will exhaust your body and your mind with his relentless barrage of negative assertions—if you let him. He will lure you in with the ease and comfort that darkness *appears* to offer. Draw the curtains, he will say. Close the door. Let the machine answer the phone, right?

Wrong! You *always* have the upper hand with the Opponent. Here's why: Darkness and the Light cannot coexist. Therefore, for every light switch you flip on, even if it's only a tiny night light, you bring hope and desire your way.

We carry great power in our souls: the power to bring ourselves magnificent, unending happiness and joy as well as the power to assist others in finding their own joy. This power manifests itself every time we apply the Transformation Formula and every time we share. Depression is a distraction. It means we are listening too keenly to the Opponent and are functioning in his realm of reaction and chaos. When we stumble, when we fall, let us truly be grateful for the opportunity to dust ourselves off and get up again. In fact, let us celebrate! For it is through falling and getting back up again that we reveal divine Light.

May this book guide you in the ways of loving yourself peacefully, radically, and entirely, and reigniting your deepest, most authentic desires. And may you turn this love into endless and unrestrained sharing with the world around you!

MORE FROM NATIONAL BEST-SELLING AUTHOR YEHUDA BERG

Kabbalah on Love

This charming little book has a simple yet profound message: Love is not something you learn or acquire but an essence within, waiting to be revealed. Buried by layers of ego, fear, shame, doubt, low self-esteem, and other limitations, the incredibly powerful force that is love can only be activated by sharing and serving unconditionally. Only then will the layers fall away and the essence of love reveal itself. The book draws the distinction between love and need, which is a selfish product of ego, and reminds us that we cannot love someone else until we figure out how to love ourselves and connect with the love within. A Valentine like no other!

The Kabbalah Book of Sex: & Other Mysteries of the Universe

The world is full of sex manuals instructing the reader on the ins and outs of great sex, but these tend to focus on only one aspect, the physical mechanics. According to Kabbalah, the key to fulfilling sex lies in self-awareness, not simply technique. Sex, according to Kabbalah, is the most powerful way to experience the Light of the Creator. It is also one of the most powerful ways to transform the world.

So why doesn't great sex happen all the time in our relationships? Why has the sexual act been so deeply linked to guilt, shame, and abuse? Why do long-term couples lose the spark and get bored with sex? *The Kabbalah Book of Sex* provides a solid foundation for understanding the origins of sex and its purpose, as well as practical kabbalistic tools to ignite your sex life. This ground-breaking guide teaches how to access higher levels of connection—to ourselves, our partners, and to spirit—and achieve unending passion, profound pleasure, and true fulfillment.

Beyond Blame: A Full Responsibility Approach to Life

"It's not my fault!"

Then whose fault is it? In his new book, based on popular and successful workshops at the Kabbalah Centre International, co-director and teacher Yehuda Berg advocates taking personal responsibility for life's problems rather than giving in to the tendency to blame others for them. Berg provides simple yet potent kabbalistic tools to overcome this negative tendency toward blaming and live a happier, more productive life.

The latest volume in the bestselling, small-format Technology for the Soul™ series, *Beyond Blame: A Full-Responsibility Approach to Life*, is a compelling guide to achieving positive change through the power of Kabbalah. In addition to practical advice and exercises, *Beyond Blame* features inspiring personal stories from people who have used Kabbalah's transformational formula to stop "the blame game" and instead make the choices that lead to ultimate fulfillment.

If you think that problems, chaos, and suffering in your life are random or caused by external circumstances, think again. Learn how to eliminate "victim consciousness" and improve your life, starting today!

The Living Kabbalah System™: Out of the Darkness™

Take Your Life to the Next Level™ with this step-by-step, 23-day system for transforming your life and achieving lasting fulfillment.

This revolutionary interactive system incorporates the latest learning strategies, addressing all three learning styles:

- Auditory (recorded audio sessions)

- Visual (workbook with written concepts and graphics)

- Tactile (written exercises, self-assessments, and physical tools)

The sturdy carrying case makes the system easy and convenient to use, in the car, at the gym, on a plane, wherever and whenever you choose. Learn from today's great Kabbalah leaders—Kabbalistic scholar Yehuda Berg and Instructor Jamie Greene—in an intimate, one-on-one learning atmosphere. You get practical, actionable tools and exercises to integrate the wisdom of Kabbalah into your daily life. In just 23 days you can learn to live with greater intensity, be more successful in business and relationships, and achieve your dreams. Why wait? Take your life to the next level starting today.

God Does Not Create Miracles. You Do!

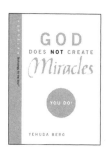

Stop "waiting for a miracle". . . and start making miracles happen!

If you think miracles are one-in-a-million "acts of God," this book will open your eyes and revolutionize your life, starting today! In *God Does Not Create Miracles. You Do!*, Yehuda Berg gives you the tools to break free of whatever is standing between you and the complete happiness and fulfillment that is your real destiny.

You'll learn why entering the realm of miracles isn't a matter of waiting for a supernatural force to intervene on your behalf. It's about taking action now—using the powerful, practical tools of Kabbalah that Yehuda Berg has brought to the world in his international best sellers *The Power of Kabbalah* and *The 72 Names of God*. Now Yehuda reveals the most astonishing secret of all: the actual formula for creating a connection with the true source of miracles that lies only within yourself.

Discover the Technology for the Soul that really makes miracles happen—and unleash that power to create exactly the life you want and deserve!